Simple Landscaping

Sustainable Construction
How to Do More for Less

Fred Swisher

Published by
Incubation Press
Bend, OR 97701
866-839-BOOK

Simple Landscaping
Sustainable Construction
How to do More for Less

Copyright ©
November, 2010 by Fred Swisher
3rd Printing, March 2015

Edited by
Linden Gross
Bend, OR 97701

Simple
Landscaping

Sustainable Construction
How to Do More for Less

Fred Swisher

To my wife, Sarah, with whom I spend so much time in our work and home. It could be easy to take her for granted. I don't. Sarah helps and supports me in so many ways it's impossible to quantify or even fathom. She is a hugging champion, the one with the big heart and a great woman on the rise. I love you, Sarah.

To my friend and writing coach, Linden Gross. Linden has been behind the scenes on both my landscape books. Frankly, without her these books would not be worth a damn. Linden's cool head and professionalism have saved the day more than once. Thank you, Linden.

Lastly, I dedicate this to a good friend, Bruno De Block, who died tragically this year. Even though I will never get to read the book that he never wrote, I am motivated by his love of thinking and learning.

Fred

Contents

Introduction

When you find the answer it will be simple.

— Robert R. Updegraff

Simple Landscaping is the result of the right approach. Based on three key ideas. Unify by creating connections, honor the sense of place and integrate yourself into the work. I promise that viewed with these three lenses, it will be revealing. These ideas impact your results just like finding the right tool for the job does. Call it a mindset for success.

Most people underestimate landscape construction. It takes more than a pick-up, shovel and a strong back to succeed. Landscaping is also a bigger subject than most people suspect. Notice a few of the wide variety of "Scapes", hardscapes, waterscapes, mindscapes, webscapes, naturescapes, seascapes, rockscapes and plantscapes. Landscape is a "macro" concept. It includes many elements.

I'm an old landscape contractor, but am still learning new ideas and methods. I build landscapes for a living. Being a landscape author is really only possible because of so many mistakes (mine and others) I've had to learn from. I take pride in my projects including this one. The three most important ideas that have proven out over time for me are the subject of this book.

- **Expansiveness**
  – reaching out with design to include the surroundings and context

- **Authenticity**
  – keeping it simple, natural and real

- **Doing it right**
  – respecting the process, involvement in the outcomes

I started landscaping at age 14 here in Bend, Oregon (Sunriver). Before that, around age 5, I wanted to be an astronaut or a garbage man. By building with recycled on-site materials and designing expansively in my landscapes, I guess I have been a kind of explorer. I've been a contractor for 35 years. Earlier in my career I did several remodel projects as a builder. Today I'm most often busy fixing poorly done landscaping (still remodeling).

In Bend during the 70's, lawns surrounded by juniper shrubs or mugo pines were prevalent. Landscapes were minimal at best back then. Spaces outside are "by definition" landscapes, but many of them were just left to their own devices and looked pretty rough. Today, plant material and design choices are much broader. More importantly peoples' preferences have finally shifted to favor low maintenance and at the same time more functional projects.

As with all big projects, prioritizing and planning are keys to success. In this book the intent is to make that as simple and as easy as possible. "It doesn't take a sledge hammer to break an egg."

The potential today for great outdoor spaces is the best I've ever seen. Let me take you on a brief tour of my landscape universe. We'll consider vital and innovative strategies that will definitely enhance your project results. It's amazing what can be done. Natural landscaping requires less maintenance, but also costs less than traditional design. The money saved on upkeep over the years often adds up to more than the full cost of construction! By recycling on-site materials into the landscape and also creating more functionality, savings will surpass 50%. The resulting discounts aren't at the expense of either art or quality. Frankly, the common "old school" style landscape was foolishly wasteful. Perceptions are changing but a couple of core complimentary values always drive dollar decisions. Spending money efficiently and refraining from destroying our biosphere will always be important.

This material isn't only a theory or an idea too far ahead of the curve to be useful. These are proven methods to help you through the process. Your landscaping work is a reflection of your learning. Call it an experience continuum – all of us are somewhere on it. Recognizing our own strengths and weaknesses is important because knowledge is power but only if we apply it. Ultimately, repetition is the mother of skill and everyone can learn from their own mistakes. Still, trial and error learning is overused. This book will point the way for you to learn sooner and easier. Besides, I have learned a ton from my own mistakes (and by fixing the mistakes of others), let my loss be your gain!

It's the intention of this book to help transition to smarter and healthier landscapes. Let me know how I've done if you have questions, comments or complaints. Visit our website BendPineNursery.com for other books, events and contact information.

It's amazing how fast things have shifted these last few short years. I offered a generous guarantee back in 2010 that reading this book would save anyone building a landscape a lot of money. From the hundreds of copies sold not one person was dissatisfied with this claim. Really it's a no-brainer, once you think through the ideas presented in this book you know right where to go to save a bundle on your project. I'm still excited about these ideas and concepts that are often worth thousands of dollars. I know you'll agree that it's worth a good look, before you get into landscape construction.

The ideas in this book were developed in the high desert of Central Oregon, but the concepts apply universally. I've consulted and toured other regions' landscapes and these concepts are the same even if some construction elements differ. Simple is often hard to achieve and takes some thought. Let me help you in these pages.

For a local approach here on the high desert with design and plant choices, you may be interested in my first book with my partner and co-author Sarah Whipple – *55 Myths, Tips and Secrets*. It also has a design questionnaire, lists of resources and is organized like an almanac with easy access for your specific questions.

My third book *Top 10 Traps: Landscaping Wars*, out Fall 2015.

PART I

EXPANSIVENESS

If you want to be a big-picture thinker, you will have to go against the flow of the world. Society wants to keep people in boxes. Most people are married mentally to the status quo. They want what was, not what can be. They seek safety and simple answers. To think big picture, you need to give yourself permission to go a different way, to break new ground, to find whole new worlds to conquer. And when your world does get bigger, you need to celebrate. Never forget there is more out there in the world than what you've experienced.

—John C Maxwell

Chapter 1

Sanctuary from the Ordinary

*All our problems stem from not being able to
sit quietly alone with our thoughts.*

—Pascal

When you have a good family photo you want to frame it. If the particular photo means a lot to you, you'll probably upgrade to a nicer frame. Why not think the same way about your landscape, since it both frames and enhances your home? Even more importantly, a well-crafted landscape provides you with a retreat from our over-stimulating world. Such a landscape is an extension of your home and your life that ultimately brings you joy.

Most people—whether professional landscapers or not—forget or neglect two critical points about landscapes:

- Landscapes are alive.
- Landscapes are dynamic and non-linear.

Your house won't grow by itself, but your landscape will. Your house won't evolve by itself over the years, but I guarantee that your landscape will change. Builders, God bless them, usually make terrible landscapers because they bring a right angle/straight line mindset to a landscape's asymmetrical reality. As I write this, I am revisiting a landscape I have worked on several times in the last twenty years. The trees are much taller and a few things need to be removed. My clients, the Hepworths, are at a different stage of their lives and therefore have different requirements for their landscape. Like a dynamic sculpture that is never really finished, their landscape has matured and improved with age, but now must adapt to a new set of circumstances.

I think most of us would agree that living someplace with character is preferable to living in a house surrounded by a cheap-looking, non-functional yard. These generic landscapes—which don't respond to the native environment or the owner—simply cover things up with sod, irrigation and nondescript plantings.

Making your place connect with both nature and you, the owner, is the goal. A landscape done right will also provide a sense of place. But the ways to clog up a landscape with materials and plants are nearly endless. Let me give you an example. I like using rock in landscapes. Some rock can even be considered furniture. I've built fire pits and set rocks and boulders to use as tables and chairs. Rocks bring in an element of the earth that nicely balances the space between building and plants. Many consider them "the bones of the garden." In many cases, however, rock use falls flat because instead of looking natural and being functional, it becomes one-dimensional. Instead of being *of* the earth, it's simply *on* the earth. Rock wants to hold a hill or be like the mountains in the distance or the river rim. Rocks are seen in big macro natural settings. So connecting the rock work, giving it a bigger context, is important.

Another mistake often made using rock is having several types rather than what was native. Using a single type of rock like river rock or Basalt can provide a simple and elegant landscape backdrop.

A great landscape is simple to understand but hard to do. Take a problem site, expand its possibilities and reveal its true nature. Make sure to respond in the authentic "voice" of the place. You must find its "personality" and build from there. If you don't, you wind up with a generic cookie-cutter commodity.

Expansiveness is anything that rescues one of these orphan landscapes and builds in some life and interest. Here in the U.S., we tend to build houses and to some degree landscapes in a building-block style. If you doubt this, look around at all the retaining wall block that is now used. These stacked cement block walls never look natural and mostly are just a cheesy afterthought. They are really the opposite of expansiveness, because they chop up the place. To expand the aliveness of a site you need to connect with the surroundings, especially if you have a great natural feature or a river, lake, canyon, or city view.

The key for me here is the art. The art and science of landscape boil down to getting the people who live there and the essence of the place to work together.

Why can't your gardener or maintenance person handle this? In landscaping just as in any other profession, there are three levels of skill. First you've got the laborer who does no thinking and simply provides the physical manpower required for the job. At the second level is the craftsman, from apprentice to journeyman, with skills and some specialties. Finally, there is the artist, the one with vision, the bigger thinker. The artist brings the physical, the technical and the creative to each project. That's what sets him or her apart.

Let's take using a chain saw as an example. A laborer can use a saw to cut fire wood, tree limbs, or whatever is required. A craftsman can take it a step further and fell a tree right where it needs to go so that it misses buildings, power lines, etc. An artist can do those things, but can also carve a sculpture or totem pole from the tree. These three roles aren't always respected and problems can obviously arise when you use a laborer to do technical jobs or when you bore an artist to tears by having him do nothing more than manual labor.

Even though my body is the most useful "machine" I own, I'm too old to want to just work physically at landscape. Still, the skill sets I've picked up over my career definitely come in handy. The fun part for me is perfecting the process itself and enjoying the ride from project to project. Education is never-ending. Just like in art school, I see a change in my work and develop a keener focus as the terms and projects change over time. I am continually transmuting design and modifying techniques. The flow of new ideas and lessons learned from recent projects is endless. I'm lucky because each project is part of a dialogue I get to have daily with this art of landscape.

There are plenty of ways do landscapes wrong, including being an egotistical artist. That takes the zest and excitement out of building an outstanding landscape. I want to make the construction process work for everyone, not just me. That's why I stay onsite until project completion. This minimizes delays and construction messes. I realize that this is important for everyone to feel safe and for ideas to flow best. Jumping back and forth between jobs is a game someone with a big crew and overhead can play. I want to concentrate and be able to give my best effort to the project at hand rather than float between several job sites. On bigger projects, I've learned this lesson the hard way, but I've got it now. "Be like a postage stamp," said Henry Wheeler Shaw. "Stick to one thing until you get there." I believe in that.

I use the indigenous materials found on each site as materials to build with. The mess left by home excavation and development gets cleaned up and reused. Recycling and using materials, plants, and items found onsite is cheaper, better for the environment and, ultimately, simpler than the alternatives. Rocks, if artfully set, become a powerful element in your landscape and involve no maintenance. Dirt utilized from the site is obviously cheaper than paying for material to be trucked-in or out; it's also not full of new weed seeds to deal with later. This kind of recycling gives immediate tangible returns, and is easy to fall in love with now that money has become even dearer to us as consumers.

Using what's indigenous (native) also does something even more special. Louis Kahn, the great modernist architect, talked about construction elements expressing the essence of themselves in the construction design solution. By integrating elements from the site to rebuild and remodel the place itself, the process and elements can shine through. This gives the final product a sense of wholeness and integrity that can't be achieved by merely applying "store bought" materials.

I remember a quote from a course in miracles I attended several years ago that applies to site restoration. "The holiest place is where a past hatred becomes a present love." In this case, holiest can also be interpreted as wholeness.

Yes, I'm biased. I love beautiful landscape, and I build landscapes for my living. But even if I didn't have this background, I would still see places I hate. Places where nature is trashed. Landscapes that people won't go into or that they can't use, even if they wanted to. Many sites are just plain and unnecessarily ugly.

What gives me my thrills and kicks is to attack such a place and transform it. Using the methods I've mentioned and others I'll talk about later to make it whole and all of one piece gives me great gratification. Putting a landscape together with these concepts is like solving a puzzle. By using a kind of alchemy of the place, the final product can appear more natural than it did before.

This transformation means more than money or beauty or even dare I say simplicity. I love knowing that I got to rescue a wasted space and make it into a place that fits the owners and the environment. It's a privilege to be part of the process that helps landscapes become alive, useful, and enduring. It's human nature to fix problems and explore new solutions to old problems. Landscape is no different. Fixing the little stuff, like an entry upgrade, building a fire pit, or similar projects is still fun to me because each job is different. But to make a landscape whole even if all the details aren't completed is even better. It's a kind of deep cleaning and elegant remodel that turns landscape from commodity into art, and makes it a new day for the place as well as its owners.

These transformational landscape makeovers can happen surprisingly quickly. In a matter of days or weeks, an ugly, non-functional yard that for years has been bothersome to keep up or just downright weird can be converted into a simple, natural and balanced sanctuary.

Eliminating what's not the work of art is the first task. A little like the sculptor who chips away at a piece of marble in order to reveal the beauty within, you must also develop—and then retain—a clear mental vision all the way through. That's the most important part of the landscaping equation. Finally, you have to get from point A to point B and get the job done, which is the hard work part.

These three components—expansiveness, authenticity, and process—working together give a visceral jolt to a project, and provide a transformational experience.

Idea: Expansiveness isn't only about bigger or more money. Enhance the natural lines. Expand and extend shared spaces and views.

Chapter 2

Lifescape

*A cup's value comes from the space that holds
liquid, not the clay it's made of.*

A landscape is a little like a nest, clothing, or even a second skin. We eat in our landscapes, often bathe in them, and sometimes sleep in them. Our life extends through our home and into our landscapes, which tell a story about us, just as our clothes, hairstyles or cars do.

In short, your landscape is—or should be—a lifescape that's shaped and designed so that it's an extension and reflection of you and how you live. People are different, and their landscapes should be too. If you don't want to spend much time outside, why automatically opt for a lawn that will cost you in terms of time, money or both?

On the other hand, if you're the type who wants to live outside whenever the weather permits, figuring out what exactly you want to do when you're out there will dictate many of your landscaping decisions. If you want to go outside to take a break and get away from it all, a grassy lawn won't be a sanctuary, but a grove of trees or a fire pit can be. Having a landscape in which you can congregate or to sit and enjoy a view gives you livable spaces compared to a big lawn with no real use unless you have kids and/or dogs, or like playing croquet, horseshoes or tag football.

It doesn't help that the majority of lawns wind up looking pretty ugly, and don't really fit the place or enhance the structure of the building. And yet generic landscapes continue to revolve around lawns, with no thought given to who will be living with them or whether they'll ever get used. Nobody would live in a house where the rooms have unusable space, so why build landscapes that aren't functional or attractive?

It boils down to a false choice between using your landscape to enhance your own lifestyle or keeping up appearances to pacify your neighbors. The fact is that a landscape can look good and function well, too. That's why I enjoy building and living in custom lifescapes instead of generic landscapes.

A lifescape respects both the owner and the environment and goes far beyond the generic-style landscape. What you desire—in terms of livability as well as maintenance—is as important as what assets the site offers. I have clients who just want to look out certain windows; that's how they want to "use" their landscape, as a foreground for the view. Knowing this, we tailored the design to work for them and with the site. Since their place was very native and natural already, it only took minor changes to rebalance the site with the home and upgrade the inside views of the property. This particular client can and does watch the deer around her water feature through her kitchen window while at the sink.

Since landscaping is consumed just as much from inside the home as from outside, you want to consider how it's framed in each window. Of course, many clients want to live outdoors, throw parties, and get the kids out of the house, so how you use the landscape is just as important as how you experience it visually. You might opt for a fire pit, rock patio, fancy entry, outdoor dining, functional lawn areas, native grasses, tub, pool, water feature and/or shower.

Like a used car or a new Rolls Royce and all the choices in between, landscaping is not only one thing. There is a continuum from light touch to complex and expensive in landscape choices. Understanding where you and your family are on this continuum is critical before you dig in and do the work required.

Next, look at what you have to work with in terms of site. When you start a landscape project, you develop a plan first and then shift to logistics and distribution. People and materials are directed to the site. In the middle of the project, tracking and support systems are keys to successful outcomes. When you are finishing up, it's time to handle the final clean up and punch list items. A little extra effort to hose down the street and sweep the curb and sidewalk will make an immediate difference. Don't "poison the well" at the end of a project by leaving trash lying around or calling it good and neglecting to complete all those small, finishing tasks.

As you work through a job, you'll be constantly removing and eliminating structure to create a new form. The old school had the excavator doing most of this kind of work. The modern green and sustainable school uses heavy equipment, but also uses what it removes to fill, top, and replant with. Of course some junk onsite may need to be removed; that may be the safest, easiest, or healthiest option.

By all means act as the janitor or cleaning lady of the site. But remember that during this clean up phase, you'll probably find valuable material. For instance, if you must take a rock wall out, ask yourself where you can reuse the rock. The old wall is probably coming out because it wasn't right in the first place, so most likely some of the rock should just be used for fill or be removed. Keep the good rocks for use later. Some plants can easily be transplanted; others can be buried and left to compost where appropriate. Sometimes dirt can be coaxed out of a site and you won't need to bring in topping material. Just keep in mind that the less clutter you keep on the job site, the better the recycling opportunities that will reveal themselves to you.

To build up your landscape you will need to add. However, if you add more than necessary, you'll be throwing money away. This is one simple zero sum reason for using what is onsite already. Recycling this way can save you thousands. Once you've run out of materials onsite you'll need to pick what to bring in next. Here in the high desert, I like three materials best: ¾ minus (road base) gravel, screened material for top grade and compost for planting. Rock might need to be brought in, so definitely think twice before removing it. New trees and plants shouldn't sit around, so plant them when they're delivered rather than holding them onsite.

Your ultimate goal is to accomplish these three things:

- Remove—and possibly recycle—what's not working.

- Decide what needs to stay, making sure that machines or people don't hurt it while accessing the other areas.

- Add recycled or trucked-in material, including new trees and plants, irrigation, sod or seed, hardscape products, boulders, and whatever else you need. This should be your last step. Bringing in materials before recycling and not protecting native areas is the one sure way to throw your money away.

Finally, consider your timetable as well as your finances. Sometimes, people want to complete their landscape immediately, while others need to take an incremental, layered (though not piecemeal) approach. Those of you on tighter budgets and not in a hurry can use the season to help. Winter can let soil settle, for instance, and spring is a good time to seed native grasses and wildflowers.

The key is to have a vision and a plan, and then to proceed in that direction. That's exactly what the Keskis, who have a Lindel cedar home on two-and-a-half acres, did. Their property posed landscaping challenges. The lot was large and built on top of a little hill. Indeed, the driveway was steep enough that in the winter snows people had slid into the ditches along it more than once. This was really an excavation issue that hadn't been dealt with at the time of construction because landscaping funds had run out. The house was about one third of the way from the main road into the lot. At the edge of the parking pad and upper driveway, big rock piles and "unsafe" holes chopped up the space and made driving to and from the house potentially even more dangerous.

The clients had tried twice to take plans drawn by the two largest landscape companies in town and come up with a realistic budget. Both plans called for over an acre of landscape of mostly lawn with full water. Neither plan addressed the excavation issues or a handful of other eyesores including a misplaced propane tank on a rock outcropping, the drain field in the middle of the proposed lawn and a very small planting area at the house's entry.

Both plans were nicely drawn and cost well over a thousand dollars each, but neither solved the problems that needed fixing. In addition, both specked a backyard three times larger than the front yard, something that none of their neighbors had, with access limited to a narrow path.

My response was to flip the entire scheme on its head. After excavation and fill had been completed to make the driveway safe, the lot was graded to connect it to the "back forty." Instead of landscaping an already beautiful native area replete with cool twisty junipers and moss-covered rock outcrops, we cleaned the grade, seeded native grass and put in a fire pit. The result is clean and striking.

The grandkids love to play in the natural forts and the landscape is super low maintenance. It's simple naturally.

We didn't stop there. We made extra room for an entry feature. We relocated the propane tank (using a rock saw to hide the piping) and worked the front landscape around the drain field. Along the driveway, we built a small berm to which we added rocks and larger trees. This helped blend the house and the site, and the now beautifully landscaped driveway provides an opportunity to view and enjoy the place as you drive in or out. Now instead of giving mixed messages, the landscape helps the house really fit the site.

This project is a great example of "do less of the non-impactful and unneeded work." Instead, focus your attention and budget on what really needs doing to make the whole place work. In this example we did a significantly better job than either standard landscape proposal could for about half the cost. And the maintenance costs are a fraction of what they would have been with either of the other plans. More importantly, the landscape worked with—and improved—the occupants' lives. It wasn't just a landscape, it was a lifescape.

A lifescape is shaped and designed to fit its inhabitants, with useable spaces that bring *you* into the equation. During the design—or redesign— process, always consider your own needs and preferences in addition to the landscape's bones. Landscape is not just a commodity; it should be a resource to enhance your life. Older people won't use their landscape the same way a young family will, so the design should fit the occupants. If you have a love of nature, why not create a place for yourself in it that fits your preferences instead of opting for the same old thing? People with a small home and a big lot who want to be outside can take advantage of the outdoor space to expand their living possibilities. Conversely, someone who is out of town a lot and wants freedom from yard work will have another set of design ideas.

Don't make the mistake that so many make and assume that you can deal with the function of the place later. For your landscape to fit and reflect your lifestyle, it can't be an afterthought. Participate up front so you can design and build a space you belong in. Our environment affects us more than most of us recognize. When you have a landscape that truly fits you, your environment supports your lifestyle as well as your wellbeing.

You also don't want to make the mistake of framing the dialogue about your landscape with what you don't want. Many of the people who hire me or attend my speaking engagements initially tick off their requirements for their landscapes. The list includes getting rid of the dust, no weeds, firebreak, a fence, a green lawn, low cost upfront, low maintenance, plants deer won't eat, no bugs, and on and on. None of these are elements they want, but rather things they don't want in disguise.

Landscape has many more possibilities than keeping problems at bay and maintenance low. Here are some considerations to help you figure out what you want from your outdoor space:

- Show off your property's assets and bridge the indoor and outdoor worlds by inviting the outside in (minus the bugs, of course). If you can see from inside the house into the landscape, you've already got some visual connection, so physical connection is an easy next step. Even better is to have a visual hook that pulls your attention outside the home, like an arrangement of trees, a flowerbed or rock garden feature. A water feature can be seen from inside and heard from outside. Using a device to connect the two realms helps balance out your place in the world. Decks and patios can be built with this transitional quality in mind so that they become zones or layers rather than barriers.

- Use landscaping to increase privacy. Trees can be planted to create natural screening in specific locations around the perimeter of your yard. When neighboring properties taint your style and enjoyment, screening these views softens them and sometimes eliminates their effect on you.

• Create a living landscape. Most of us buy a house because we want to live in it. The next step is to extend the living space and experiences out into the landscape. If you have kids, dogs, or are caring for adults with disabilities, you can create spaces for them outside, too. Don't forget to create your own space. A garden with artistic characteristics, or even a vegetable garden, is just the start of what else can be done outside. In the micro world of your landscape, you can bring in modernity or not. The barbecue is the outdoor kitchen extension we are most familiar with. Hot tubs take the bathing outdoors, and can even be set up for outdoor television viewing. Patios create living space. These sorts of outdoor rooms allow you to connect with the natural spaces, and allow you to have a different kind of experience outside than you do inside.

• Consider functionality. Design choices are usually made before you buy your house, but even with an existing landscape you can make small changes that lead to big improvements. For instance, adding a hardscape—an area built outside that is level and solid—can make the difference between spending time outside or not. You can also eliminate daily annoyances, like cramped driveways that are hard to navigate. In many cases, all it takes is shaving away a little lawn and adding some gravel to provide buffer space for easier parking and turn-around.

• Accessibility—the ease by which you can enter and leave your house—is another essential component of livability. Steps and railings in a path leading to an outdoor space will limit its use. The more steps, the less traffic. I know this to be true from personal experience. I wanted to be able to walk from my deck to my native lawn with no steps separating the two. Once I made this construction change at my own house, I immediately used the deck and yard at least four times as much as before. Of course, some spaces don't lend themselves to this kind of modification. In those cases, make sure the steps are safe and located in the optimal places.

• Consider what kind of maintenance you want to commit to doing or paying for. A new green lawn where there was dust and a mess a few days prior seems like a great idea at first. The color and smell of bark chips also compares favorably to the dust and debris before it. Throw in a couple plants and wow, your yard really looks better right away. Compared to the chaos of a construction zone, these kinds of projects look good. But compared to what's really possible, they are often a joke. Sure, having a lawn is—or used to be—part of the American dream. These lawns require regular maintenance and literally tons of water, which is even more of a waste since they often don't get much use. Compared to a landscape you and your family and friends can actually do things in, a high maintenance, non-user friendly lawn is pretty silly.

Here's an insider's secret about landscaping and the great American dream for a big lawn. The business model for many of my landscaper friends is to build that big lawn landscape and get a check, then maintain it and get lots more checks. Designing with lots of maintenance built in means someone is going to have a job cutting, fertilizing, thatching, aerating and keeping up the lawn. Do you want to be that somebody or pay for that somebody?

Personally, I hate to mow lawns. Long, long ago, I realized that maintenance just meant more work and more pain. I also figured out that approaching work as hours for money was less important than the fact that it took time away from more fun activities I could do instead. Another vote for low maintenance.

Like me, most people I meet want low maintenance landscapes, because when you run the numbers, mowing, fertilizing, watering and winterizing can cost thousands per year. This is a big reason why I've embraced native low maintenance in my design.

We don't need to go out and conquer nature. At very least, we don't need to fix nature's settings and features. On the other hand, we clearly do need to fix most of man's attempts at outdoor construction. I'm living proof that you can make a career out of that. The trick is to invoke nature and also find useful rapport with it. This can be as simple as using smaller lawns and native grass to minimize expensive watering. Compare that to a big lawn that requires spray-head irrigation (non-drip irrigation). The lawn is like having a Visa card with high interest and the native landscape is like owning gold—it just keeps going up in value as it matures. That value isn't just monetary. Landscapes affect your mood and mental state, too.

A landscape, however, needs to do more than enhance its inhabitants' lifestyle. It should also improve physical health by being organic instead of relying on pesticides and chemicals. Preoccupation with the color green can be toxic to people and pets. Maybe it's lucky that so many people never use their lawns.

We have been brainwashed by commercials that fertilizers and toxic pesticides are a necessity, but that's a lie. A lifescape that emphasizes low maintenance—and uses compost and drip irrigation to water only what you run the emitters to—can reduce disease problems and all but eliminate the need for chemicals. It's a matter of balancing the maintenance with the lifescape.

In contrast, a xeriscape that's 100 percent native doesn't consider people as part of the equation. How realistic is a desert landscape along a row of track homes or in the Safeway parking lot mediums? I applaud the extensive use of native plants and water-saving techniques, but let's be real—we use the space, too.

By opting for drip irrigation for plants and trees, and natives grasses with plenty of good organics used as substrate for the roots of the grasses and plants, you get the best of both worlds. You conserve by using only a fraction of "normal" water use. And because water goes directly to the plants you're trying to grow instead of the weeds you'd rather not, maintenance weeding is significantly reduced. These techniques allow for a much wider range of design choices to meet the needs of us, the occupants, and the resulting landscapes end up looking and feeling better, too.

All too often, however, clients don't wind up with feel-good landscapes that work for them and that fit their lifestyles. I often hear clients say that the prior landscape company didn't provide the landscape they thought they had commissioned. Excluding the crooked element as in any business, this usually stems from a mismatch of personality and livability with design. The result? They don't feel good in their space.

If you still doubt that your environment has a strong effect on you, try breathing underwater or having a picnic on a freeway. Okay, not really. Still, I challenge you to take this seriously and release yourself and those you love from poor design habits and typical status quo design choices. A great landscape context will add life to those who live there. Customizing it with your lifestyle in mind and connecting to the natural elements are two steps most often neglected. This robs many people of a better quality of health and enjoyment that a lifescape with real livability offers.

There's no way around it. If you are putting in a new landscape or redesigning the one you have, you have to identify how you want to live in and with it. The way to approach this is like a brainstorming session. List your ideas of what you want and how you like to use outdoor space. Would you love an outdoor space where birds or frogs will gather? Plug this into your list. I like to have a place to read and catch some sun a little ways from the house. If that works for you, add it to the list. My wife Sarah and I have an in-ground trampoline the kids love; you might rather have a pool or pond. There are lots of choices outside; the point is to make them intentionally.

Don't edit yourself or let anyone else edit you during this list-building exercise. Just put everything that comes to mind on the paper. When you have written down all the obvious easy stuff, ask yourself "What else?" Now come up with around 50 percent more. Then you can call your list good. Next, take a break and set aside the list for an hour or a day until it's time to edit it. I repeat, don't edit while you brainstorm or let anyone else correct your ideas while generating your list. Only edit yourself after the fact.

If you honor this process, I'll bet you'll come up with at least a couple design aspects you would have almost certainly neglected that really fit you and your lifestyle. Plugging these new insights into the overall design will serve you and give you more livability and more pleasure in your lifescape.

Nature can be a church, a business, a fun zone or an escape, and it's our home. In the end, it's all about figuring out how you want to live in that outdoor home, and then making that work within the space you have. Customizing a lifescape that meets your lifestyle needs is just the first step.

Idea: Landscape is a sculpture you live in, an extension and reflection of you.

Chapter 3

What It's Worth

Don't trip over dollars to pick up nickels.

I've seen so much money wasted on landscaping projects over the years, I could recommend trading commodities as a safer bet. Betting is a pretty bad idea when the odds are against you. In fact, more than 80 percent of my work involves fixing other people's mistakes. If you are going to make a good decision about what to do with your landscape and who to hire to get it done, you need to know how to go about the decision-making process. You'll be well served by a holistic perspective.

First and foremost, you need to compare apples and apples. To my taste, this year's new honey crisp variety is really the best, though there are plenty of good apples out there. If you don't like your choice all that much, you can always make applesauce. Of course, landscapes cost a lot more than apples and when done wrong are nightmares that you wind up having to live with. So you need to get your landscape right the first time—or at the very least the second time if things didn't work out so well initially. But that's not as easy as it sounds. I looked at a project that had been done several times and was no closer to being right than it was at the outset. Fixing it would have required starting all over again.

I like the movie *Groundhog Day*. Bill Murray keeps waking up to the same day and reliving it over and over. The only twist is he can make better choices in various situations each day. Finally, after he gets to the core of how to live, it's a new day and he can start fresh. Of course the storyline is fantasy, but this particular flight of imagination has a bit of truth that relates to the subject of landscaping. I'm amazed, for example, at how blind we can be to what's in front of us. I guess that explains why so many landscapes are merely mediocre, plain or underutilized. An awful lot of landscapes are experienced only cosmetically, but the owners still pay plenty to maintain them.

Expanding landscaping value is getting more for your money than you would have somewhere else. Ultimate beauty is loving the project's result. Low maintenance is being able to live with your property and not having it own you in terms of time and money.

When you add up all the space devoted to lousy landscapes, you come up with a very big number. Americans spend billions on landscapes. Now that fuel and travel are pricier and discretionary funds scarcer, fixing up the home front is gaining appeal again. But if you are going to spend your dough on expanding your landscape's possibilities, you want to make sure you get the most for your money by making informed decisions.

As I've discussed, expanding doesn't necessarily require space or money. If you have no budget, just cleaning up a place expands it. If you can squeeze a few dollars, a small budget used correctly can make a big difference. Maybe you have a special feature or vista to develop or an unwanted view to obscure. Making the view from your property more appealing doesn't cost much and yields big rewards on both the personal and financial fronts. Thinking of selling your house? Enhancing the entry will expand its curb appeal. Upgrading this small area will give you major bang for your buck.

Instead of spending impulsively, utilize your investment of time and money best by simply expanding your ideas and understanding the options you already have. Once you determine what's possible, also plug in the ideas that best suit your unique situation and lifestyle. There is nothing wrong with competing with the Joneses, if you raise the bar first.

Therein lies the challenge of landscaping. Or should I say two challenges:

- You're buying something not yet built.
- Human brains have a very hard time accurately imagining anything that they haven't experienced.

Maybe you've heard of the little experiment where the subjects watch a basketball game and are told to count passes between players. A guy in a gorilla suit runs on the court, but only one third of the test subjects "see" the gorilla, even though he is right there. Now imagine how many customers can really see the landscape they're commissioning, which doesn't even exist since it hasn't been built yet. This means that in most cases people really don't know what they're getting. Over years of dealing with clients and fixing landscapes butchered by others, I've found there's a big gap between real and imagined outcomes.

As I've mentioned before, the focus on pictures and images is a real comprehension problem and can prove to be an expensive mistake. I often bid on projects that are an acre or more and sometimes have wells. When one such prospect wanted a large lawn, I suggested a drought-tolerant variety. Because of the well, I proposed that the size of the irrigated lawn should be modest, with native hardy grass incorporated next to the spray irrigated lawn areas and supplemented with organic compost to help it thrive. I suggested using natural boulders to enhance the surrounding native landscape look and mountain views. Rocks need no water and provide interest. Besides, since there was a big beautiful pile of rock just beyond the proposed lawn area, the customer would not be paying for either the boulders or for delivery. The only cost would be for setting the rock.

I spent time showing my prospective clients similar landscapes and explaining my concept. In the end, someone else's bid price was "substantially" less (20 percent) than my complete proposal. At first glance, this cheaper bid would save the couple several thousand dollars. However, closer examination revealed problems with this "competitive bid." Most notably, the proposal had five times the lawn area with a sod blend that uses more water. Wells don't last forever and when the water goes so will their landscape.

What they got—an oversized lawn and a well destined to dry up—isn't like the picture they imagined while in the buying mode. The cheaper bid only covered 70 percent of the entire area needing a fix, so the project still doesn't look finished. The buyers made the mistake of comparing only cost and not taking advantage of resources onsite. Resources such as their premium boulders now can't be used or set because moving them would harm the new lawn and irrigation. Because the homeowners skipped several steps in their planning and implementing, at some point they will have to start all over again.

The problem is that in the age of consumerism, we are all trained to buy packaged products. Most people don't shop for empty space or think of uncovering space, they think about filling it. Recycling isn't as popular as shopping—just look at how many cars are parked at the ReStore and how many are parked at Costco. Since landscape is more complicated than it appears on the surface, buying a landscape is not unlike buying a used car from a salesman trying his best to confuse you. As a result, too many people spend money they don't need to on landscapes that never deliver their potential.

We are all consumers. Consumption is an ultimate drug, and marketing bombards us 24/7. Selling tactics hypnotize us. No one I've dealt with yet has said, "I have extra money and feel like wasting some." Yet we all spend—and often waste—our money, frequently simply to get that chemical high inside our brain.

Being American power consumers also means we are in a constant arena of competition for our money. That triggers the dilemma of choice. In the landscape business we compete with RVs, travel, cars, boats, timeshares and remodeling for consumers' cash. In addition to all these honest businesses, we also compete with the not-so-honest ones—the "all sizzle and no steak" types that sell but don't deliver.

Something doesn't have to be of real value to be sold as if it is valuable. I was recently walking down the street in Vegas and got talked into attending a "presentation for time shares." After ninety minutes, I turned down the deal and went on my way with a "free" gift. The thing that surprised me was that almost 50 percent of the other people at the presentation bought a timeshare for $15,000 or more. We had all just been walking down the street, not even thinking about timeshares. But these folks plunked down their money just the same.

Most people purchase timeshares on the spur of the moment because they buy into someone else's story. Real value, however, entails getting more of what *you* want, rather than what a slick salesman wants you to buy. Doing upkeep instead of enjoying your landscape, for instance, takes the fun out of it all and diminishes the value. Getting a lot for what you spend isn't value if you really didn't want it in the first place or have a hard time keeping it up year after year.

We need to look past the hype, but that's hard to do. Ask someone to tell you why they bought a new car. The answer usually is reliable transportation for "getting around town." What really motivated them to part with their hard-earned money to buy a $40,000 SUV? They bought it because of easy financing, self image and, similar to all those timeshare owners, being sold. At least you can re-sell a car, since it's a finished commodity when you purchase it. A landscape is built in layers and stages, however, and may never be finished in an acceptable form. We all love a good deal, but if our premise of what we are buying is false, the process and the result will be flawed.

The good news is if you look at the metrics you can make sound decisions without falling prey to emotional tricks. The key to buying anything—and especially a landscape—is getting what you need and want. Don't short-circuit the process of communicating your expectations up front openly and honestly just because of the high of the buy. Otherwise you will either spend more than you need to or you won't get the quality you could have.

Money wasted on landscaping usually happens by doing unnecessary things, doing it wrong, or using a bad contractor. So if you're not doing the job on your own, you also want to make sure that the contractor you hire is legit, liquid and competent. A good talker but a lousy doer can cost you thousands more to fix and complete an unfinished job.

Landscapers don't offer cash for clunker deals or easy to get financing like car dealers do, and landscapes aren't destinations like New York, Vegas, or Hawaii. But unlike vehicles or vacations, landscapes, if done right, will hold and increase their value while providing daily enjoyment. If you have a place connected to nature, you can enjoy the seasons, sunsets, and sunrises right in your backyard. Having a spa, fire pit, or some other version of outdoor living space can provide unlimited mini holidays. And since you won't wind up driving as much because you like staying home, you'll save money there, too. By extending your livable space, you will add value to your home both in terms of appraised value and livability.

Unfortunately, most landscapes miss this opportunity. As discussed earlier, generic, over-simplified landscapes don't connect and expand, they merely cover space. Landscape isn't really just another commodity. Generic landscapes don't deliver the power and impact of an artistic environment customized to your needs and preferences.

Making something special out of a generic landscape, however, is harder than you might expect. Track developments feel and look a lot like an open sardine can, with cookie-cutter homes that usually have the front driveway and the entry to the house right on top of each other. The job is further complicated by the lack of space and neighbors within reach (sometimes literally).

I had one of these places myself, which I was desperate to unload so that my wife Sarah and I could buy property that could accommodate all the trees we have in our nursery. The housing bubble, however, had just collapsed. Besides taking a steep financial hit, generic houses had to offer something special for them to sell at all. In my case, I had dressed up the landscape and made the best out of its parameters, and in the end, the landscape wound up convincing the buyers to take the house.

The first thing to deal with when almost every window looks into a corresponding neighbor's window is increasing the privacy. Most of these developments have six-foot high fences. The eye line of a human standing up is usually just below six feet, but most houses aren't a single story and most grades have higher and lower areas. You end up seeing the fencing, along with yet another square box of living space and all the neighbors to boot.

Start by marking the offending views, then pick and plant trees as appropriate. Evergreens are best if the views are direct from inside the house. Deciduous are better for screening the patio and outdoor living spaces, but don't forget to factor in the sunlight. In the summer, shade is wonderful, but in the winter you'll want light to get through. Sometimes you'll have to compromise your choice of trees and partially block offending views with leafy trees to avoid blocking out the winter sun.

Outdoor living space is the next place to consider upgrading. Generics usually have some kind of token patio off a sliding door in the backyard with a postage stamp-sized lawn that no one uses. But a patch of grass that serves a purpose, now that's something different. I installed a small lawn that went up a little berm, giving the illusion of a hill sloping toward the back of my small lot. I pushed out the patio space so it could actually be used as a living space. Planted pots and a small fire pit gave the bigger patio visual interest and suddenly my backyard became an inviting garden to be in. But without blocking out the view of the nearby neighbors, it wouldn't have worked.

I also changed the walkway to the front door by moving out the path that ran alongside the house so you no longer had to enter into a tight corner. Using a little rock and shade-loving plants, I turned the space that had been the walkway into a tasteful planter. And instead of leaving what would have been a tiny lawn, I planted perennials, shrubs, and a few specimen trees, which gave the house curb appeal and softened the garage-dominated front.

Dressing up this cookie-cutter landscape landed me the sale during a terrible real estate period and despite tons of inventory on the market. The new landscape brought out the true nature—and the best—of the property, and also provided a canvas onto which the new owners could put their own stamp.

If there were a secret to never doing anything superficial I'd share it. The truth is, it's a constant challenge. We must take the time to look below the surface at the whole picture. I have turned down several projects and lost out on proposals when that wasn't possible. It isn't because I'm rich or don't need to earn a living. But in my world, when people insist on something being done wrong, it's not worth it to help them fail.

In one case, a customer wanted a water feature that would be seen for only five seconds as you drove up to his property. You wouldn't even see it as you left. To build a $10,000 feature that you hardly see is just plain goofy. Placed near the patio or next to the entry, it could be admired from inside the house as well as when outside. If it had served to mask road noise, an out-of-the-way location at least would have proved useful. But this was a case of imagination blinding intelligence.

Enthusiastic or not, skip steps and you lose, guaranteed. Landscapes usually cover thousands of square feet, so they ultimately cost thousands of dollars. After rushing in with ill-considered notions, the biggest mistake people make when investing in a landscape is comparing price when they should be comparing value. It doesn't matter how good a deal rock and dirt are if they're not needed in the first place. Similarly, if a bid for a project comes in at a third off the competitor's quote but doesn't cover the entire scope of work, it's not a fair comparison—or much of a bargain, either.

Sizing a project is a must for comparing bids, but so is function. A landscape is a collection of outdoor rooms, each with its particular requirements. Each outdoor room in your landscape should have its own purpose. Bark chips and sod lawn aren't going to give you that. Neither will black plastic covered with river rock or cinders.

Finally, remember that expenditure doesn't end with the construction—maintenance and reliability will cost money, too. How many mistakes do you want to fix later? How much should your yearly upkeep be? A landscape investment decision is not easy, but by taking it seriously you will improve your return on investment, not just in terms of your real estate value, but also in terms of its use and your enjoyment.

Idea: True quality brings value not only to your bottom line, but to your life.

PART II

AUTHENTICITY

"Only do, what only you can do."

—Thomas Dolby

"It seems the simpler you are,
the better things work"

—Louise Hay

Chapter 4

Revealing

Truth passes through three stages—first ridiculed, second violently opposed, finally accepted as self-evident.

—Schopenhauer

These days more and more of us are vacationing at home instead of on the road or abroad. But to have a vacation in your backyard, you need beauty. Mimicking a photo isn't going to get you there. You have to conceptualize based on who you are, your needs and the true nature of your surroundings. We've already explored the lifescape aspect of this equation. Now we need to launch an external exploration, which by definition involves looking outside ourselves. In a later chapter we discuss places to look for inspiration and vision. But your own backyard has its own natural spirit waiting to be recognized and/or uncovered.

I recently surveyed a remodel job where the site's dirt had been scraped bare and the area was starting to turn weedy. Asking the owners their intention and looking around the one-acre property revealed a simple fix. Out back away from the house and road, I spotted over two thousand clumps of native fescue bunch grass. The neighbor's lots also had this native grass growing in abundance. It was early spring, a perfect time to transplant. We dug up about half of the clumps of grass from the unused back area and planted them around the front that had been excavated during the remodel project. We also added more native seed blend and some organics to build up the soil a bit and cover the seed to help it start.

Looking around the site, we also discovered some beautiful rocks that would go to waste where they sat. We used these boulders to build rockeries and create settings for plantings, giving a native and an elegant touch for focal areas. This native rock proved perfect for framing the entry.

The clients had wanted something nice but had no desire to create maintenance. They also weren't sure if they would end up living there long or might rent it out, so this solution fit their lifestyles as well as their budget. Both these free resources revealed themselves by looking at the native landscape, as well as the neighboring yards, and taking some time to survey what was available onsite that could be used.

Discovery is about noticing something that was unseen before. Copernicus and Galileo helped mankind realize that the earth was not at the center of the universe, but yet we still say the sun rises and sets. Hubble expanded our concept of the universe in the 1920s to go beyond our own Milky Way galaxy. Only fairly recently did we finally figure out that an asteroid hitting earth caused the dinosaurs' extinction. That there are in fact other planets outside our solar system was only proven within the last two decades.

In short, just because we think we know something doesn't mean we do. A secret about landscapes—or more specifically about the nature of weeds—revealed itself to me about five years ago. While I was hiking into the wilderness areas of Mt. Jefferson, I noticed lots of dogs, horses and people—but no weeds. It wasn't because of a lack of weed seed; the animals I'd just seen had carried plenty as I'm sure birds and native animals had before them. I looked more closely. There were native groundcovers, an abundance of different flowers, and plenty of trees, but not a single weed. No one was secretly pulling them and herbicides weren't being applied.

This new insight, coupled with work I'd done in the past with new lawns, fire-damaged sites and, of course, excavated lots, gave me a new way of looking at weeds. Weeds drive most of us nuts and we declare war on them. But weeds like cheat grass and knap weed are really pioneers that start a natural process to reclaim a barren piece of land. Faster-establishing grasses, then more permanent grasses, bushes and trees follow. Though we Americans think in terms of packaging and instant gratification, nature evolves and seeks balance. What I realized on that walk into the Jefferson wilderness is that once that balance is achieved, weeds naturally disappear.

The goal in a native landscape isn't to fight weeds, even though I'll pick them and occasionally use Round Up. The goal is to promote balance. The faster you provide the environment with the dominant long term plants it favors, the sooner the weeds become the bit players they should be. In town you may never totally eliminate every last weed because most of your neighbors are still fighting weed wars and dumping chemicals into their landscapes. But with the right choices that work with—instead of against—your property's nature, you may reduce weeds by a factor of a hundred. The key lies in discovering what that nature is.

When you design by discovery rather than using pre-planned, pre-packaged, pre-determined design, you must remain open and observant. I've found that even on some of the simplest projects I contract for, I never catch all of the details the first time. I can spend a couple hours examining the site and questioning the owners, and I'll still miss things on the first go-around. There is a kind of "what else?" mindset that prompts me to search for what lies underneath whatever isn't working, to get to the bottom of it. Out of confusion, the real nature of the place begins to reveal itself. To really understand something new, let your mind stay open as long as you can and then sleep on it. Most often we only make incremental progress, but added up these small steps can create significant insights.

Even after listening to the land's quiet but powerful voice, going back to the site multiple times and speaking with the owner or occupant more than once, I still won't catch everything, but I will flush out enough to see the bigger picture of the place before a design proposal is written. Recently, for instance, I met with prospective clients for nearly two hours. After listening to their lifestyle preferences, walking the site and looking out from inside the house, I realized what was needed for them. They had three areas that required work—the entry, the backyard and the rock outcroppings. Once finished, the place would be more private, more inviting and downright spectacular.

Great landscape design reveals and highlights the best qualities of the home it surrounds. The particular strengths and opportunities of the property, once uncovered, can be taken advantage of, and the weaknesses and problems can be neutralized.

Revealing the inner landscape is similar to coaxing a shy person with talent and something to say out of his or her shell. Each place has buried treasures or hidden assets. You just need to look at and listen to the environment. Consider all the sensory options. Planning on building or fixing a water feature? Play with the flow and how the water is cut by the weir rocks. You can use options in construction to create optimal sound characteristics and a full range of sound that's pointed at the desired living space for maximum effect. A place in the yard will often call out for a water feature, a new focal point in the landscape.

Going out into nature (mountains, beaches or rivers) to observe will help you reveal other secrets of elegant design. Then go back to your property, walk the site and sit with it until you begin to see what to highlight, what doesn't belong, what needs help, and what needs to be added. If you establish this kind of rapport with nature, you'll know that you have the inside track into the authentic identity of your own specific environment.

You'll never get this from trying to copy a photo of someone else's landscape. I occasionally like looking at the ubiquitous landscape pictures, as well as before-and-after photos, but they are a poor substitute for firsthand, out in the landscape experiences. Steal ideas from these books, use the principles they teach. Just don't fall into the trap of trying to copy your project from a picture.

The root cause of most landscape construction problems is mistaking superficial images for what works in the real world. Even master landscape photographer Ansel Adams embellished his photos. The map is not the territory, so don't just project a mental movie onto your site. Camp out on it, have a picnic there, at least stop and sit so that you can watch the way its natural elements interact. Where does the sun comes from? Is it windy? How's the soil? Is it rocky? Where do you and your family tend to gravitate? What stirs you? What features do you dislike?

Having an open mind is only half the equation. You need to live with the place to have any chance of really understanding it. Like other life forms, a site is alive. Listen to its essence, explore its dimensions. As you eventually learn to tune in to its frequency, your property will reveal possibilities and even a personality, just like a person does when you get to know him or her. Overlaying a generic plan onto a living site without revealing its inherent qualities is like having a relationship with a "Russian model" on the Internet. It's not real. If you approach the design of your project with an open, questioning mindset, the character and potential of the place will reveal themselves.

The alternative to designing by discovery is to relinquish the task of planning to your landscaper or designer (or worse yet, have no plan and no concept at all). However, if the person or company determining the plan hasn't looked at your site, doesn't know the people living there, or doesn't design by discovery, the resulting landscape won't reveal anything indigenous. The quality of the place itself will get covered rather than honored.

Much like a visit to a dentist, revealing the ins and outs of your property will identify latent problems. But once revealed, problems and their siblings—opportunities—are the building blocks of great design. This is why revealing the best design takes repeated visits and conversations, especially since what gets revealed changes with the seasons. No design is perfect, but by listening and observing year-round, you will connect with what is really there and figure out how best to work with your property.

Answers to questions don't just reveal themselves. You have to work at the process and be willing to listen, look and learn. It's not easy to dig a little deeper, especially when you think what you have done is enough. But remember: staying open and probing into the subject helps create the most successful landscape projects.

The Taylors' landscape, like so many, was literally a diamond in the rough. The couple runs horses on half of the acreage that adjoins the house they recently bought. The place had been built in the late seventies between two of the largest rock outcroppings on the property.

Becky's favorite place on the property was their private backyard where they had added a new deck. The deck is well built, but there was no way to safely step from the deck into the yard. With the mini excavator, I built up the grade to create an easy step off the deck and into the landscape.

Next, we had to fix their landscape, which didn't flow and was "confused" as to its purpose. With large properties, cutting up the space takes away all the fun of having all that land in the first place. We removed an unwanted view that blocked out a very desirable and picturesque setting. Now the view includes a cute red barn, native grass field and horse pastures in the distance, thereby honoring the sense of space.

The place also needed a big haircut. Mugo pines and aspens had grown up against the house's pre-existing wrap-around deck and were dying off slowly. Dead or dying trees don't do any good for a landscape so we removed the hopeless ones. We also thinned out a couple large aspen that rubbed against the deck and edge of the roof, more for structural and safety reasons than for fire prevention.

The rock outcroppings were surrounded and covered with scruffy natives and some old leafy trees that because of the watering had "volunteered" over the years. These days mossy rock is golden, so we revealed the natural features of rock by removing the untidy over-growth.

Once we exposed the rock and grade of the site, we polished up the property by taking out redundant cosmetic borders (like wood poles along the lawn) and barriers including stumps and rock piles. We dressed up the entry with plantings and boulders to match up with the natural rock outcrops. Finally, we graded out an old garden and a spot next to the driveway to create a single large area that we seeded with native low-maintenance grass.

To make the most out of this landscape, we had to take away more than we added. Each time a layer was removed, we'd notices other opportunities to remove more old junk, including an old playhouse, as well as a fence. When we finally "got to the bottom of it" and could see the character of the property that had been hidden underneath the overgrowth, we had to build and rebuild with landscaping to bring all its components into harmony and natural balance. The result was a restored sense of place that was three times as spacious, and yet even more private.

Idea: Reveal the gifts that nature gave the place.

Chapter 5

Connecting Elements

*I saw an angel in marble and carved
until I set him free.*

—Michelangelo

A good landscaper is like a combination housekeeper and seamstress. First, the housekeeper needs to clear away what's not working. Then the seamstress comes in to sew the various pieces of old and new fabric into a stunning whole.

Nearly all landscapes I see lack that sense of being connected and "all of a piece." Even if the mess that was there before has been cleaned up, if you look with a critical eye, like somebody doing an archeological dig, you notice separate zones or projects. These weekend warrior "I've got an idea" projects get scattered around the site and it shows. Added up, they don't equal a connected landscape. It's clear that the work wasn't done at one time or wasn't conceptualized into a comprehensive plan. Contrast this with a natural setting in the mountains along a stream. The stream is an element, the trees, shrubs, and ground covering plants are all elements, but they fit seamlessly.

"I live on a street and in a town with houses all around, so how can my landscape be connected?" you ask.

Good question.

I ask this same thing of people who want a xeriscape-style landscape. None of us lives in a vacuum. Our landscape has to reflect and acknowledge the surrounding features and elements before it will feel right. Thinking conceptually and starting with the big picture of your setting are critical for success. You need to determine what you have to work with first and then apply proven techniques.

Take a project I'm just finishing as I write these words. The Schefflers bought a bargain house, benefiting from the opportunities created by the real estate crunch. The previous owner hadn't paid attention to either the landscape or how the houses nearby were being built. The neighbors had raised their lot level behind Diana and Larry's narrow backyard by several feet, and built a two-story house. A six-foot fence only covered the foundation. As if that wasn't bad enough, the backfill at their house was clearly the cheapest the developer could find. The grass "growing" in this fill material looked terrible, too.

The Schefflers' house is built on the end of a cul de sac so you enter through "the wrong end of the funnel." With nothing to compensate for the narrow entry, the house looked like it was an afterthought to the road. On the north side, leafy trees had been planted for permanent screening, but this isn't how leafy trees work in the winter. And overall this landscape didn't have a square foot of connected space.

These kinds of non-landscapes are so common they don't really shock us. Most people are unaware of what a landscape can do for their home and living experience. They just think that they're stuck with whatever is outside of their house. The realization of its deficiencies hits when they sit on their patio and watch the neighbors eat dinner or watch a TV show in the house next door. Their outside experience becomes whatever is happening inside their neighbor's house. Another clue that their landscape doesn't fit and connect with the natural elements comes when all they see is a fence and sides of houses. While the pattern of a development is an element and you need to acknowledge reality, don't think for a moment that working with nature is optional. A landscape is for people to use and appreciate, but it only works if it also reflects and connects with what's native around it.

We replaced leafy trees with conifers on the north side for year-round greening and screening. We moved the leafy trees to the south side for summer shade, taking into account that they'd drop their leaves in the fall, allowing far more sun exactly when dropping outside temperatures make the extra heat desirable. At the sides of the entry's narrow funnel, I placed boulders and planted bushes to give a sense of bulk as well as a "gateless gate" to pass through when entering and leaving the driveway. As for the lawn, we eliminated half of it, and took out the rest and started over. With the new lawn, we added an inch of compost and used a tougher blend of sod.

The elements we added—gravel, plants, trees, pavers, and planting beds—matched the color, shape, and type of what was already there. The finished landscape is simpler. It works for the owners' lifestyle, which includes two large, friendly dogs. It mirrors trees found around the neighborhood, and the native ponderosa pines used serve as desperately needed screening. Grass in the small front yard helps the property tie in with the neighbors' bigger lawns, but with its new personality, the landscape now elicits lots of compliments.

Bigger properties need landscape love too. A project involving an old farm of slightly over forty acres had hidden assets including a blocked mountain view, a pond and literally tons of moss-covered rock. Because of its size, the budget didn't allow for doing the whole project in a year. So we picked priorities.

The old farm house must be over fifty years old and hadn't been sited to catch the big mountain view, so the owners decided to build a new residence. Picking the best building site was one task. Reworking the driveway that had utility boxes and even a water weir right where they could be hit by a truck or driven into during winter storms, was another. The driveway entry also needed fixing, as much for safety as for aesthetics.

This site had rock substrate underneath, capped by just a foot or two of dirt and gravel. To change the driveway grade by much, we knew we'd have to bring in fill and gravel. But we kept that to a minimum and maximized the use of the materials budget by working with the lay of the land (or in this case the rock under the land). The trick was to take down the high spots where rock poked up into the existing driveway and flatten the base rock substrate as much as possible without using an expensive rock hammer. By flattening down the high spots and applying gravel, the driveway is now one clean plane, instead of being bumpy, with dips.

By following the flow of the existing rock, we used far less extra material and the driveway fits the site even better.

The grade determined the retaining wall level. The retaining wall holds the terraced elevations, frames the space and makes the landscape look good in the process. To build the wall, we recycled the property's big pile of moss-covered rock and also used the rock left from field clearing and excavation of the driveway.

The entry at the main road was fixed by relocating the utility box for the phone and building a boulder buffer around the exposed water weir. We also used gravel to gently bring up the level of the driveway to that of the main road. To eliminate the driveway's sharp right angle, we cut into a short hill, which we retained using boulders. This accomplished two important things. It connected the entry with the middle of the drive visually, while making the driveway approach work and look even better.

Since the driveway continued to the future building site where we had built the big retaining wall, the rock boulder feature was like a spine or thread that pulled the place together from the entry to the new house pad. It also simultaneously framed and reconnected previously disjointed parts of the property, showcasing its assets that are now visible.

Before the work, the mountains had been obscured, as was the big pond on the drive in. Now the beautiful distant view is a feature and the existing pond feels like part of the landscape again. Discovering what was already there and honoring that with a connected landscape re-established a natural sense of place.

Here are a few of my favorite connecting techniques:

The first simply involves grading the land so there aren't holes, dips, edges or lumps. Even if the unevenness isn't obvious, kneel and examine the terrain at ground level and you'll discover how rough and bumpy many sites are. When I install lawn, I go to a corner, squat down and with my face just a foot or two off the ground, I look across the area being graded. That shows me the high and low spots. A wide rake helps to smooth out the bumps and dips. This same technique should be used to smooth out and fill holes on the rest of the landscape, though you may need heavy equipment for larger areas.

During this process, I also use fill to bring the grade up to where it should be instead of building unneeded steps and retaining walls. If you can raise the landscape grade so that it's closer to hard surfaces like decks, patios and pathways, you eliminate work as well as unnecessary stairs. I want the lawn to be at the same level as the concrete slab patio. I only want one step going up to a front door if possible. This grading and filling technique connects the lines of the place and makes it easy for the eye to follow. It also makes walking around the place safer and easier. The alternative is an undefined grade that looks unnatural because it doesn't really fit with the lay of the land. Unfortunately, most often contractors and homeowners skip this important filling and grading phase altogether. To compensate for poor or nonexistent grading, they use steps and retaining walls that cost a lot and detract from the landscape. Though going back later and cleaning up the grade is a lot more work, this is often the best way to fix a needlessly complicated site.

My next connecting technique is great for the high desert. Use drought-tolerant fescue grass. It's a thinner-blade grass that thrives in the drier areas. It also won't suffer damage from lack of water like bluegrass lawns do. This kind of fescue (also called bunch grass) is naturally patchy, but won't ever look brown or burnt like the sod blends can. These drought-tolerant fescues can be used for normal looking irrigated lawns too.

The ostensible reason many people buy bluegrass blends is for more color and traffic. If there is that much traffic, put in a road. As far as color, fescue is in fact green. Bluegrass does fill in better without reseeding, and most landscapes with lawns use it. The problem is most people expect it to remain consistent like a carpet. Without extensive maintenance, most lawns don't really work out that way.

We get calls every day from people wanting alternatives to high maintenance (read high cost) lawns. This is it. My own home lawn gets cut once yearly and we use a pre-existing irrigation system once a week and only during the hot summer months. This kind of fescue has another great benefit—as it get established it pushes out unwanted weeds.

Drought-tolerant fescue also works great in transitional areas between "normal" lawns and native areas. Feather out the fescue clumps, tapering the uniform grass into an asymmetrical pattern as it goes into the indigenous landscape. The overspray from the lawns irrigation is enough to make these areas thicker than they would be with normal rainfall, which helps transition the space smoothly from manmade into the native topography.

In the Bend area, you can't buy sod with only this type grass, so we are forced to grow from seed. You won't get the instant gratification of putting down a sod lawn, but if you time your project with the seasons, you may not need a permanent irrigation system either. I recommend using a hardy fescue blend, supplemented with a hose and sprinkler as needed, and being patient while awaiting germination. In most cases, this will save you several thousand dollars. Individual bunches of fescue grass can also be planted—you can buy them in one gallon or smaller sizes at many nurseries. Or, if you get permission, you can dig them where plentiful, since they're the one of the easiest and hardiest plants to transplant.

To sum up, follow the line of the surrounding land, then simplify the grade and smooth it out. Once you've improved your grade, plant bunch grass (or other natives) in similar patterns to the surrounding natives. That will help you multiply connecting elements and start creating that seamlessness that gives you a natural-looking and functioning landscape.

Rock is a great no-maintenance element that can help connect and transition from the house to nature. Except for bodies of water and meadows, the bigger natural landscape around us is not often flat. So if you want to connect with nature, you need the bones of the garden instead of more flatness. Use retaining stacked rock walls, rockeries, and simple arrangements of boulders to give a landscape structure. Of course, you can also add water to your landscape and even copy the native meadow look.

I use big trees to blend foreground and background, since they can hide unwanted views. But rocks offer something even more permanent and durable. They can create a three-dimensional structural connection like trees, but with a fourth dimension. They can become part of the place, part of the substrate, from which trees and plants can emerge.

Using rock from the site in question is the best when possible, because the indigenous quality of a site's boulders automatically adds to that sense of connection you're going for. If placed artistically, the results can be very powerful.

On the other hand, boulders themselves often just look like big rocks, not all of which are worth using. Like collecting treasures at the seashore, you don't bring home everything. You pick and choose the best, and then display those judiciously. That's easier said than done with heavy boulders and rocks that have to be moved with the right equipment to be set artistically. Not everyone knows how to do that, so you need to find the right help if you want the best, most natural-looking results.

Giving your landscape that natural feel also involves connecting visually with the surrounding native context. Intentionally transition from the right-angle boxiness of the building into the patterns of the site. Nature isn't square; it's round and asymmetrical. Most houses, however, are pretty square. So as your landscape design moves out into nature with patios and decks, add angles and curves. I think this is one of the appeals of lawns; they are usually made with rounded edges. Lawns connect and fill the empty, dusty space, but at a cost.

Landscapes in this more modern design style function like bridges that link home to earth, with several overlapping and reinforcing techniques that help create a sense of wholeness. Done in this style, landscapes reflect the personalities of both the owners and the native environment. These kinds of modern landscapes live in both worlds. As inhabitants of this world, our task is to integrate both the very old and timeless with the new modern ways of life. Trees shouldn't be planted under power lines. Utility boxes need to be accessible, but can still be obscured with shrubs, etc.

The draw of the modern, however, often clouds the fact that we are still pretty primitive in many ways. I compare the shortcomings of traditional fertilizing methods in terms of effectiveness and health to a fast food diet. Neither one has good long-term results.

Like anyone else faced with putting hard earned money into their landscape, I want my plants to grow, be healthy and look good. But I'm often a rather slow learner, and slower still to make changes, so going organic seemed daunting and frankly unnecessary during my early years as a landscaper. As I learned more, I used peat moss to hold water and make the chemical fertilizers I was using last longer. Later I found that organic fish fertilizer worked better than chemical versions. But animals dug into the fish fertilizer and hurt the plant roots. Now I use compost, which is by far better than other alternatives. Once I understood that 90 percent of commercial fertilizer is wasted as it leaches through the soil, all the while creating a chemical dependency in plants similar to drug addiction, organics became the more appealing choice.

I think compost is like the Rosetta Stone for understanding the organic planting concept. It's a simple connection to a system in the real world that is already in place. Similar to the larger design elements discussed previously, it connects to what's native. In the case of compost, natural microbes live symbiotically with the plants. If supplemented with compost or compost tea during planting or yearly as a natural fertilizer, plants get re-connected and re-invigorated. Compare this to traditional chemical fertilizers used in such high concentrations that microbes and beneficial fungi are killed off. Many of these natural organisms keep the bad "bugs" away, so once plants become dependent on chemical fertilizer, pesticides (which can be toxic to pets and people) are often needed as well. This becomes a vicious cycle. These microbes were here long before chemical fertilizers, and will be here long after we are all gone. Like the sun and the seasons, we need to adjust our design to allow for—and connect with—these fixed elements.

The seasonal nature of a place also remains an important consideration. For instance, the sun will be higher or lower in the sky during different times of the year. North-facing is dark and cold, while south-facing is warm and bright. Knowing that can influence placement of everything from hardscapes to trees. As we've seen, using the latter wisely can save you money on your heating and cooling expenses, since evergreen trees protect from cold north winds and leafy, solar trees allow winter sun to penetrate through leafless branches but provide shade during the hot summer months.

Even though a stunningly large percentage of houses and buildings never take advantage of this free passive solar energy, you can still use the sun in your landscape design. Plan for the times you'll use certain areas seasonally and give yourself warm and cool alternative patios or decks so you don't get forced inside by the weather.

As a contractor first and designer second, I use proven techniques and ideas to optimally connect elements and create unity. I've always made it a point to include the people investing in their landscape in my design, much like I need to include the audience in a presentation or speech. The result is a landscape that fits into the life of its occupants and surroundings. And that is priceless. I am obviously biased from my contractor's perspective. But it's too bad that so many people wind up paying the same or more for shoddy landscapes instead of great ones.

Idea: Trees and layers of connected elements expand space and solve problems.

Chapter 6

Simplicity

*All things being equal,
the simplest answer is the best.*

—*Occam's razor*

Simplicity makes landscapes work. And the definition of ultimate simplicity in landscape entails consciously balancing the three most important factors: nature (the site), the owner, and the timeless principles of design.

Nature is going to be here long after we are gone. Ignoring this aspect in design is really the first mistake to avoid, if for no other reason than it will continue to be a mistake forever.

As we've seen, connecting a landscape to the people who use or own the property is a simple value equation. Who doesn't want to have more of their needs and wants met?

Principles of design, like the law of gravity, are ignored at one's peril. You have to think in the language of your medium. In the language of design that means composition, entry emphasis, seamlessness, and the like. This language is basically a tool of the trade. Without it, a successful outcome is pretty hard to achieve.

Blend these three ingredients of site, owner and principles seamlessly, and you'll create a place with personality and beauty. All too often, however, we simply follow our neighbors' lead and mimic what they've done. To a degree this helps connect the neighborhood. But what if the style and techniques the neighbors are using are ugly? Or expensive—either to install or maintain?

The best innovative landscaping ideas today have common sense to them because they're based on you and your property. Start there and then use the principle of Occam's razor when faced with decisions and go for the simplest option.

There are degrees of complexity or simplicity, and no absolute standard for either. Landscape in one sense is complex and needs to balance many elements to come out looking good. In another sense, how hard is it to plant a tree or shovel some dirt? The best answer may be similar to Goldilocks and the three bears. One dish is too hot, one's too cold, but there is one that is just right. Art is that way. So are high-performance athletics, or even finding the right tool for a job. All have a sweet spot, that zone where you get your best results.

Without looking at landscape construction as a problem to solve or a project with measurable results, you'll miss this Goldilocks effect. The goal is to end up with a landscape that's just right. If you opt to have a plan drawn, which can be a helpful tool for sure, remember that the plan isn't the work. Building the landscape is, and that just may not coincide exactly with what's on that paper. When in doubt, keep things simple and let nature make the call since, as we've discussed, she'll win anyway.

That's just common sense, right? Unfortunately, in today's high velocity world, both common sense and simplicity are in short supply. Sometimes simple is the hardest accomplishment. It takes thought, communication and know-how. Even if the idea of revealing nature from under the development and construction mess makes sense, for example, figuring out how to do it can prove daunting.

Modeling successful landscapes, as opposed to your neighbors', can help. I can't really cook, but using a good recipe does make a big difference. A landscape project isn't dinner, but this principle still holds true. A local guide or coach with the right experience can also help you create beautiful and useful landscapes by sharing his or her recipe or formula for success.

But to really get what you want, you need to explore your options. And that doesn't mean just looking at photographs in a magazine or a landscaping book. Visit other special places, take a seminar, go to an industry show or just relax for a while and sit.

Japanese gardens are a perfect place to inspire landscape ideas and extend possibilities. My favorite in the United States are located in Portland, Oregon. These gardens exude, celebrate, and showcase nature, framing it to create a very expansive feel. A Japanese garden pulls the viewer into the surroundings, often like a spectator at an event.

If you are a fan of Japanese gardens, you may have heard of the principle of shared space. A garden might have something like a lantern in the foreground and then a similar larger lantern placed at a distance outside the garden to connect the view. Rocks and trees can be used in this way, too. This technique visually extends the space. It makes the garden seem bigger and more expansive.

In any form of art, our eye and perception follow lines. I took modern dance in college and had a great teacher who was barely five feet tall, but when she was dancing you would swear she was over six feet. She had mastered extension. The opposite was true with me. I looked a little like a dancing duck—not even a flying one. That's the opposite of how the right lines extend your sense of dimension.

In both Japanese and Chinese gardens, you'll find a depth of elements rather than just more stuff. Chinese gardens are similar in that they integrate what's natural and tend to spotlight the asymmetrical. They pay attention to expansion. They tell a story. They are alive. Unlike Japanese gardens that are strictly ornamental, people actually lived in most Chinese gardens. They use buildings and pathways to create an inner depth.

My favorite Chinese garden is located in downtown Shanghai, smack in the middle of booming China. Walking through Yue Yuan Gardens, you see past, present and future all at once. The gardens' buildings fit into the dynamics of the place flawlessly. The details work together and provide a purposeful journey of discovery to enhance your experience. The layering of elements in the time/space continuum keeps you fascinated and involved as you walk through the gardens.

The principles of *feng shui* and the Chinese idea of *chi* both emphasize flow and circulation. Without proper movement from one place to another, a landscape, like any other art form, feels cramped and unhealthy. When the lines in a work are cramped and ambiguous, we perceive them as jumbled and small. And that impacts us emotionally and physically. I remember one unfinished landscape so poorly done that the owner and I got actual headaches from spending too much time there...until we fixed it.

When looking to expand your landscape, expanding your mind also helps. To open my mind, I take a walk or I look at all the stars on a clear night. I watch a Natural Geographic special on the earth, energy or the environment. I realize how small I am in the grand scale of the universe and even within the town I live in. By realizing just how large the world really is, I am able to appreciate that I have plenty of room to push my own landscape envelope out into the expansiveness of it all.

Expanding your landscaping doesn't necessarily mean that you have to own more or pay more to get a bigger feel. I've moved several fences or parts of them, because fences are really all about lines that can either frame a setting or divide it. Simply by removing lines that are visually constricting, the landscape opens into something bigger. But not all lines are constricting. I often use boulders or rock to create natural lines in the landscape that follow the curve of the land in order to connect spaces. That kind of connection also expands the landscape.

There are several other methods for opening up space without adding more property, some more successful than others. Lawns are very often used because they visually connect loose ends. Bringing a lawn up to the planting areas makes the landscape seem bigger than all its separate elements. The problem with this approach is that the reliance on a lawn alone often brings our focus to the foreground instead of to the features and textures of the surrounding nature. The opening act is causing us to miss the real show.

Fortunately, other tactics work far better. You can sometimes achieve that bigger feel by adding layers, especially where the view into the surrounding area is less than desirable. Tree hedges, shrub borders, rock formations, and waterfalls or ponds can expand interest in a more inward way. For a sense of how this works, just look off into the vanishing horizon and count the layers of elements. Your property—with the tree line behind followed by hills, then clouds etc.—make up the layered view.

Depending on the particular set of factors you're working with, you'll need to find your place's individual balance. Landscape views blocked by a fence can be extended out by appropriate tree placement. By cropping (breaking) the upper line of a fence with trees that are a little taller than the top line of the fence, the fence line no longer dominates the view. Adding trees also brings depth to the scene. Tying into the style of trees surrounding your property by planting similar trees in your own yard will expand the space even more by using shared space. The key is to play up a point of visual interest and downplay the parts you don't want to see.

Expansiveness can be created even when there's nothing to look at outside your own yard, or worse, when you really need to block an ugly view. To make sure you maximize that feeling of expanse you're looking for, approach the process backwards. First block the unwanted view with a tree, tree hedge or berm. Often the offending view only needs to be completely blocked in one or two places, such as from a window. We have a nice neighbor who parked his trailer against our property line. So we planted three or four large trees to block it out. But right next to that parking spot is a natural clearing, so we left that space open. If you isolate the problem, this kind of selective screening is often all that needs to done.

If your yard consists of just a fence and token lawn, you need to address that feeling that you're living in a box where something is missing. Instead of looking over the fence in the hopes of seeing something interesting that's not there, you've got to direct the line of view some other way. Start with small steps like cropping a dominant fence line as just mentioned, and/or plant trees next to square corners. These are great spots to help blend and simplify your landscape. Trees planted at corners of roof lines anchor the building into the site, and will also help eliminate the boxy feel.

I like to establish a project's context by eliminating obvious problems first. As the setting develops, you'll find the "sweet spot" in the yard most suited for your focal point of choice. At this stage, the remaining landscaping becomes more of a paint by the numbers process, because the context dictates style and function.

In cases where the whole shooting match needs to disappear, the strategy for an expansive feel is harder, but not impossible:

- Strip away what doesn't work.
- Use layers to add depth and to block unwanted views.
- Highlight the best view with an opening in the landscape.
- Have a focal point of interest with natural lines in your yard that lead your eye toward it.
- Water features are great for drawing attention, but they are a double-edged sword because most often water features are not done right. A water feature that doesn't work or is full of algae is an eyesore. Focal points like fire pits and rockeries are safer bets and cheaper, too. Your choice will also depend on your own interests and budget. You might feature a vegetable garden, a nice patio, or a sculpture. Embellishing that particular area once you've simplified the

rest of the space turns it into your view of interest.

Ironically, stripping back a landscape in order to achieve expansiveness can prove surprisingly difficult. The Bakers had lived in their great yet terribly landscaped property on the river so long they just couldn't take it anymore. Not only was the landscaping ugly, it didn't fit their needs. For twenty years, they had tried a series of small fixes, but could never really get at the problem. The site was still chopped up from the old irrigation canal rubble. Since Bob is into mechanics and machines, there wasn't much usable landscape left. And since the house had been built on a hill, what little usable landscape they had was sloped. Speaking of the house, a septic tank right in front of the entry wasn't exactly the welcome mat the Bakers had in mind. But all those combined didn't compare with the string of small, disjointed spaces that simply looked like a confused jumble instead of a natural setting or quality landscape.

In the end, I took six separate areas and tied them together into a "swoosh" of drought tolerant, low water-demanding natural fescue lawn that went from the entry to the backyard. I softened unwanted views and opened up a private space from which to view the river canyon, which also works great as a usable backyard. At the front of the house, I used boulders to protect and hide the tank (which would have cost zillions more to relocate). This created a feature out of something that had always been a prominent misplaced blot on the landscape.

People aren't motivated to hire my company because I'm attractive, young, likable, or because I'm a good old boy. They know the work isn't cheap, and because I give a comprehensive bid up front sometimes the cost is pretty hard to swallow at first. My number one guess as to why people want me to provide them with a sculptural landscape is because they have a problem that others can't fix. Maybe they have a mess of boulders left from excavation, or a safety challenge, or a series of small irrigated lawns chopped up by a variety of barriers, like what the Bakers had.

The number two reason people hire me is they understand that landscape can be a natural art form you can both live in and enjoy looking at instead of just a generic quick fix. Besides, once we start discussing the possibilities, they find that my way of maximizing the onsite resources will actually save them considerable money. In addition, the alchemy of recycling onsite resources brings out more of a landscape's authentic indigenous character.

Most people willing to invest in a sculptural landscape have seen other finished projects, many of which are over ten, fifteen, or twenty years old. The simple fact that these landscapes look natural and attractive a decade or more after construction helps people appreciate their lasting value.

I think the third reason people hire me is because I do almost all the work myself. I don't send in the laborers and check in from time to time. An artist can't sign someone else's work and be respected or trusted. I feel the same way about the projects I take on. That's why I get the results I do. Take the Bakers' project, where I blended several unusable areas into a beautiful, low maintenance yard. We created an obvious path, starting at the newly created and inviting entry, which winds to the backyard with its dramatic river view. The scale of their landscape now matches that of their driveway. More importantly, it fits the place and it fits them.

After two decades, the Bakers can finally hang out in their own landscape and feel like they're on holiday. Looking past the piecemeal construction that cluttered the underlying landscape allowed me to connect it into one simple, impressive project. I just had to reveal what was already there, but had long been hidden.

Idea: Escape information overload, give yourself time to reflect and clarify your vision.

PART III

PROCESS

Self-improvement is achieved by individuals who appreciate direction more than those who demand perfection.

—*Crucial Conversations*
Patterson, Grenny,
McMillan, and Switzler

Chapter 7

Strategy & Tactics

If all you've got is a hammer,
everything looks like a nail.

—Maslow

Many of my competitors are no longer in business. A few were crooks, some were under-funded, and others got overly aggressive. Customers might say they had poor people skills, lacked resources, or were greedy. Fair and honest practices, and quality work obviously count. However, the real essence of their failure, as well as why their style of landscape doesn't work, boils down to a common theme: not being able to solve a problem elegantly.

All the landscapes I get called in on ultimately have a problem to be solved. The owner may have no idea or a truckload of ideas of what could solve it. But there is always a reason why it hasn't been solved. Sometimes the money it will cost to completely fix it, or to fix it right, is simply hard to accept. Often, many of these projects fall prey to bait-and-switch proposals or the lowest bid. Which brings a question to mind. Would your first choice be to ride in an airplane built by the lowest bidder?

In the end, a new landscape may be an improvement, but the original problem often hasn't been corrected. Sometimes it's even been replaced by a new problem. I can't count how many people have decided to cover an unfinished area with a sod lawn to get rid of the dust, only to be stuck with an ugly high-maintenance landscape. Or the owners who wanted to add interest, so they built a cheap water feature and ended up with algae and plumbing problems or worse yet, leaks. Curb appeal is key to value for all kinds of real estate, but many quick-fix proposals treat the entry just like any other area on the site. That becomes a problem when it's time to sell or refinance.

Landscapers are generally pretty good-natured and some put on the good old boy charm. But being nice isn't a landscaping strategy; it's simply a tactic to get more work.

When lives are at stake, people pay more attention to strategy. Before World War II could be won, first Hitler had to be recognized as a big problem, a challenge due to his initial popularity. Thankfully, landscaping isn't life or death, but this same principle holds. A strategy needs to address the big issue first. In my first book, *55 Myths, Tips, and Secrets*, the third section offers project and design consultation, with questions and check lists designed to help you develop your landscape strategy.

Just like a flight plan for pilots or a battle plan in the military, a strategy for landscape success starts with a plan, not a tactic. Once the proposal has been picked through and looks feasible, you apply tactics and techniques to deal with the issues. This is not the time to get distracted by pictures, fancy drawings or websites. These kinds of individual ideas should to be considered and recognized, but not substituted for the big picture of your strategy. Without a workable strategy you'll never achieve a landscape that works for you, your lifestyle and your property no matter how much money you spend.

The story about the teacher with the one-gallon glass jar illustrates the importance of having the right strategy. The teacher places a jar in front of the class and fills it with fist-size rocks; next she fills the space in between with gravel. She then asks the class if the jar is full. "Yes," they all say. Now she sprinkles sand in between the gravel and again asks if it's full. The class is getting wiser, but not all are in agreement one way or another, so to make her point perfectly clear, the teacher fills the jar again with a big glass of water. She then asks the class what the experiment demonstrates. Some students say, "You can always get more in." The teacher listens to a couple more thoughts. Finally she says, "This demonstration shows that if you don't put the big rocks in first, you can't get them in later."

Many people start with a tactic and then think more tactics or different tactics will make up for no strategy. They won't. But a substandard strategy won't do much for you, either. You can have a two-dimensional plan drawn, with an accompanying written proposal that explains what's shown on it, and then have the work contracted out. The quick and cheap versions of this type of strategy will result in a generic landscape design that doesn't reflect your life or your personality and doesn't do much for your property or its value. Conversely, you can add design by discovery to the equation.

A design by discovery strategy requires more time to inspect the site, to talk with the owners and to generate options. The work can be done in stages, like a war fought in battles, but the big stuff needs to be done first. For instance, if a house has a real privacy problem, the tactic of using trees will fix it, so tackle the tree screening first. Once the privacy has been accomplished, the project will need irrigation upgrade work—probably drip—and attention to the effects caused by planting a bunch of trees. Then you take still another look and adjust as needed to finish the project.

The same goes for talking to people and finding out what they really need or want, because it usually takes a few conversations to zero in on what will work best for them. Facts like whether they might move soon, have animals, have a particular hobby, or have remodel plans for the future are critical to a good strategy. Yet, these are the very things that often get missed by following "the drawing or plan made from a distance" strategy.

The discovery strategy requires people who understand what they are doing and have experienced the project site firsthand, otherwise important things will get neglected not just in terms of people but in terms of how best to approach the job. In 1994, I did a very big landscape for an ABC miniseries. Time was of the essence and we did have a roughly drawn conceptual plan with a bid proposal. However, as parts of the site had rock near the surface but not under others areas, we needed to be flexible. We also needed the landscape to look very natural for the shoot, which it wouldn't have if we just put in the specified trees according to a plan. Like picking the good produce at the store for cooking dinner, we highlighted the best stuff out of the nursery and installed them in the most prominent places. We also made sure what we did blended naturally with surrounding trees and the lay of the land. Finally we put irrigation in after everything was planted and looked just right.

Despite having to finish and have everything look like it had always been there in under three months, we followed a design by discovery strategy and considered more than a mere two-dimensional plan. Long hours and concentration led to a successful completion and even a design award.

Whether tackling landscape yourself as a hobby, getting serious, or hiring out, it's pretty hard to get to where you're going without a destination in mind and a few basics. Facts matter. It helps to know that compost is not mulch, or that so-called topsoil may well have nothing organic in it. People often will do projects as therapy or because they have a little extra consumer cash, but neither of these reasons is a real strategy. So they throw money at landscape projects and all too often wind up with a big mess. This is easy to avoid with a little knowledge and a little coaching.

Landscape, just like any business, has its own quirks to be sure. One is how easy it is to start a project outside. Just order truck loads of dirt or rock and dump it in the yard or simply pick up some trees or flowers at Lowes or Costco and you've launched your landscaping project. The finishing part, however, is the real test.

I started doing design consultations over seventeen years ago for that very reason. I would visit people's property and have to help them figure out what to do next or how to complete the project. Since they hadn't done much planning, much of their money had usually been wasted. I didn't enjoy breaking the bad news then; I still don't.

Whether these homegrown landscapes turn out well or not, they almost always fall short of the finish line. Instead of completed landscapes that gel, the owners are left with piecemeal and incomplete-looking landscapes. Examples of this include decks with unusable steps in strange places, unfinished walkways, fences in the wrong places, and retaining walls that disconnect instead of connecting, etc. Saving big on wasted efforts will also ultimately cost you much more to fix, with money actually being wasted not once, but twice. You shouldn't need to remodel your remodel. Starting right and doing it right from the beginning is the key if you really want to get the results you deserve. No special deal can save you money if it's installed wrong.

Many ideas from home construction apply to landscape construction, like the foundation, the flow of different trades, and professionalism. You wouldn't build a house one room at a time (finishing, carpet, roof etc.). Instead, you hire the right profession to complete each phase. In tough times with unemployment high there is a temptation to get things done a little too cheaply. In my home state of Oregon, though building landscapes requires a construction license, lots of work gets done by unlicensed maintenance and out-of-work laborers. Many people think they are saving money and, just like gambling, sometimes they come out ahead. Besides gambling on the quality of the work, employing an unlicensed worker instead of a pro means that in all likelihood, your project won't get thought through in a strategic way. Let's face it. Hiring someone under the table is a second rate tactic, not a strategy. Why not hire an out-of-work roofer to put in your irrigation system? Licensing is one reason, but a more practical one is that the job won't be done correctly. Later, when the lawn and plantings are not thriving, you may need a pro to sort it out for you anyway.

Professionals, on the other hand, do the job right at the outset. An expert tile setter spends one hour per square foot preparing a concrete pool for tile to be set. He takes the time because he knows how expensive callbacks are. He does it right the first time, even when he knows that it would take years for any defects caused by taking shortcuts to show up. Pros know that a project done flawlessly is their best marketing. Contrast this kind of thinking with a hungry landscape contractor who puts everything into a bid to help pay his own bills, only to have his weak skill areas spoil the overall project.

Tactics, the bells and whistles of strategy, should be your strong suits, things you do the best. Unlike my ex-competitors that are now out of business, I suggest you leave the gray area skills to others. A plumber will have plumbing tools, a nurseryman will have plant selection and knowledge, and so on. I use expert nurserymen, plumbers, equipment guys, and other professionals as subcontractors. As well as being a good coordinator, I do hardscape, boulder, grading and water feature work myself. I take on projects that fit my design and skill sets; the jobs that don't make sense for me I leave for others or refer out.

Deciding to hire out part or all of your landscaping job doesn't mean that you're uninvolved. To the contrary, you need to be involved from the very start, possibly even before your house is built. To do a landscape right means starting at the beginning, just like any science or art. Imagine starting a TV program or a book halfway through? The reason it happens virtually every time with landscapes is the perceived cost savings. True, money is tight, and even more so because landscape is the last trade to finish. However, a marginal landscape is the result. Worse yet, because of poor onsite resource management, considerable money may be wasted.

When the landscaping starts before the excavation, anything and everything usable on site can be identified and saved. Native plants can usually be transplanted; boulders can be stacked for use later. Even clean dirt, bricks, compost, mulch, or other landscape construction materials can often be salvaged. By starting earlier in the process, you save money and have a better result. If materials, plants, and rock from the site are used to landscape with, they blend naturally with the surrounding place and often solve logistic and budget problems. This is a form of "pre-cycling" and represents sustainable construction in action. However, excavators commonly haul these things out to make room for construction. I know I've already made this point, but this kind of waste happens so often that it bears repeating. It's not unusual for people to pay to have rock removed, only to have to then buy rock to landscape with. This holds true for plants, fill and other materials as well. Because the contractors want to get started and the clients don't usually know what to look for, thousands of dollars go out with the trash.

Unfortunately, it's not the norm to take a raw piece of ground or even a building site and start the landscape first. By the time "landscaping" begins, a lot has already been cleared to make room for building, driveway, and installing the development's utilities. Hardscape—like patio construction—is a typical entry point to start landscaping. So the idea of working from the ground up, of being able to control the building process from the beginning then into a finished product is unlikely. As move-in time nears, the last thing most people—especially contractors—want is more delays, so landscape quality suffers as a result.

But you don't have to live with mediocrity. The Richards' project up on Awbrey Butte was a study in the alchemy of using what was already onsite to recreate the place itself. In the end, after re-setting and removing a few hundred tons of boulders, only one half-ton pickup load of small rock was actually removed from the site. I had to order just twelve yards of gravel and ten yards of dirt. We ended up with a stunning landscape in which all the problems had been successfully addressed.

Living on a hill gives you great views and opportunities to landscape in dynamic ways (like terracing). Before we showed up to take on this job, however, Katie Richards went to stand on what looked like a solid rock, only to tumble down the hill after it dislodged. She only got a scrape and a bruise, but it was obviously not a safe arrangement for guests, kids, or even the road below. In addition to the safety issue with this property, in terms of the landscape's design, nothing connected and access was very limited to the backyard.

A poor landscape takes the fun out of a house with a great view and good location. The good news for my clients in this case was that the massive amount of boulders left by the builder could be recycled. Much like a mining operation, there was literally $20,000 worth of rock just sitting there. The problem was that it was in the wrong places. These were mostly large multi-ton boulders so we had to use machines big enough to handle them, and set up with rubber tracks so as not to hurt the pavement.

To start the job, first the rock was sorted in terms of quality. Because the site was on a steep hill, round boulders could only be used as fill, but not for the retaining wall. The small rock was also used as fill. Rocks with at least one good side and flat pieces that could be used for decoration or steps were stacked separately.

Once the boulders and smaller rock had been sorted, we began the remaining excavation. This meant taking the grade down and back, so parking could be added and the functionality of the driveway improved. Originally, the house and garage were tightly fit into the hillside lot. Once the work had been completed, instead of only being able to back down the dangerous driveway, there was room to turn around in front of the garage. We also created a place to park a vehicle and an RV storage area. We even excavated an area for an outdoor shower, and provided better retaining from the hillside. Then we upgraded several other areas with improved boulder choices and settings for stability and aesthetics.

We fixed a big problem for less than half of what was expected. As a bonus, because we used what was indigenous, it blended naturally. So we got the best of both the excavation and landscape worlds.

Translating an inspiration into a final landscape—or better yet, lifescape—requires help understanding the territory first, then help doing the work. You have to start somewhere, and the beginning isn't always pretty. Most of us want to start right out with the building, when eliminating is really required first for success. Ending up with a result that enhances your life and your property takes a strategic syntax.

I've always focused on construction and problem-solving in my landscaping business. The difference today is rather than having a big crew and lots of overhead, I enlist client and more subcontractor participation. With a win/win focus, even though work is secured through bids, everyone is more co-operative and the projects go more smoothly.

My first landscape book and now this one embody this same idea. If the process is effectively communicated, we'll all be on the same page regarding opportunities and challenges. I've found that sharing knowledge about landscape work creates synergies that raise the level of the final outcome. Like it or not, we are all teachers and students for each other.

Idea: A landscape plan isn't just a blueprint; it should be based on a solid strategy.

Chapter 8

Gettin' 'er Done

To know, and not to do, is to not really know.

Eventually, all the tactics in the world won't add up to a thing if you don't jump in and get your project physically underway. Every year we all take a stab at our New Year's resolutions. Why wait till January 1st to set a goal? Goals have power because they frame the desired result with deadlines. Saying you want to build a landscape "someday" is psychologically not the same as saying, "This is the year it'll get finished." A goal is like a making a contract or a promise with yourself.

A goal with a timeframe will naturally lead to formulating a plan based on your strategy. If we took the world's best field goal kicker and blindfolded and spun him around on the football field, without knowing where the goal was, hitting between the uprights would be almost impossible. Translate all this into building a great landscape by first seeing where you are going with it; knowing the territory. Next, when you step up and start committing to actions and investments, stay focused. Keep a sense of the big-picture result you want. As Stephen Covey has said, "Begin with the end in mind." Take the time to know where you want to go and what you can reasonably expect to achieve before running out and doing small projects.

The step between thinking it and doing it is a big one. Once you're ready to jump in, even incremental progress will get—and keep—the ball rolling. However, even a relatively small landscape project will often take massive action. Expect that failures along the way will slow progress at times on big projects, because they will. If things aren't working out after an extended time, go back to your goal and your plan and review your expectations. Projects have a life of their own; things you hadn't considered before may present themselves. If you stay alert you can fine tune your plan and goal as you continue to make construction progress. If you have carefully thought out the project, you'll find professional help as needed to solve your short-term setbacks. Keep thinking, but don't stop working. Do as philosopher Henri Bergson suggests: "Think like a man of action, act like a man of thought."

Keep the final result in your mind's eye. Have a clear proposal, a sketch or a partner you brainstorm with. If you don't do the work yourself, make sure your contractor isn't distracted from the original contract. Either way, your job is to keep the project moving until you arrive at the final result you planned. So don't hurry, but don't delay. Accomplish something each day, and piece by piece your landscape will come into focus as you imagined it. Remember, the longer projects take, the more they cost.

My own house and accompanying tree and plant nursery are a great example of landscaping in process. The lot, which slopes up slightly from a hairpin corner and gravel road to the house, is about two acres. It's a beautiful setting with giant Ponderosa pines towering over the property and throughout the woods. The property has good visibility because it's on a sharp turn on Baker Road, so close to the road that several vehicles crashed into the corner of the lot prior to us landscaping it. The road isn't going away, but recognizing the problem made a solution possible. Instead of wasting one third of my property as a buffer for vehicles failing to negotiate the turn, as the previous owners had, I built a large berm. We used the additional space behind the new berm for nursery storage. In addition, we get to use the berm to plant examples of what we have for sale. By revealing a problem that wasn't going to change (the road) and recognizing our need for nursery space, the new demonstration/protection design revealed itself as a perfect—and striking—solution. In this case, berms are the tactic and maximizing the use of space is the strategy.

When Sarah and I bought the property, there was no defined entry and several piles of dirt had been planted with grass around the site. We cleaned up and reused the dirt and boulders from the site to build the berm along the road. While doing so, we cleaned up and graded the lot flat. Now a gentle drive passes between the nursery and the house. It naturally divides the two areas while also making for easy access. To buffer the dusty gravel road that borders one side of the property, we make our compost, store materials along it and provide parking there for the nursery.

Further up the site is a building we are transforming into a store, office, storage and some growing area. We even painted our big nursery logo on it. The nursery itself covers about an acre. We group trees together in size and species categories. We have a section of seconds where it's always a garage sale with trees selling for as little as $1. But even in the busy season, thanks to the way we deliver and install, only one or two clients might come out to the nursery on any given day. So we have developed the nursery landscape over time to support our needs.

Still, running a business alongside your home brings certain concerns and challenges. We need to be able to keep an eye on things from the house, but then we want the house to be private, too. The personal and business areas need to visually connect so people can tell where to find us if they pull up unexpectedly. So we opened a middle ground between the nursery and the house where people can sit on benches or their kids can jump on our in-ground trampoline. For our own privacy, we created an area alongside and behind the back of the house that can't be seen from the nursery. That's where we do our outdoor living and host guests.

Just as for any house, but maybe more so for our situation, the entry is the most important part of the landscape. This is where customers decide to do business with us, so first impressions there are even more vital. We use our entry to show off our collection of specimen trees and our landscaping skill.

Our revamped landscape meets both our personal and professional needs. By simply rethinking the lay of the land and revising what was already there, we turned problems into assets and transformed both the look and the function of our outdoor space. It worked because we completed a thorough discovery phase once we had lived with it for a while. So we knew exactly what we needed to do.

Once you've made your plan, you (or whoever you hire) should prepare the context first in order to create the foundation for your landscape. Like a tooth that has to have the bad part taken away before it can be filled, many sites need excavation before rebuilding. Most landscapers and homeowners often skip this step. When it is left out, time and money get wasted trying to hide the underlying poor structure of the site. In the end, these kinds of projects look wrong and don't have the same expanded usable space that properly graded sites do.

It took me many years to really get the hang of shaping sites to both work with nature and create a livable environment for the owners. The spatial dimension simply can't be added later. You have to build the "platform" for the landscape construction itself. Establishing the foundation's location, grade level of a building, and how you integrate with the site is really important, because the final grade of the living space will affect your use and enjoyment. The longest journey starts with the first few steps. In landscapes, that's grading the site first to establish optimal setting levels and location.

Like getting married to the wrong partner, going ahead and building on a poor foundation will give you trouble as the project goes forward. At some point either you or the next owner will need to fix it. Whether it's concrete, plumbing, lawn, plants or whatever else, it's a nightmare to start over. Redoing a poorly installed water feature or pool will cost twice as much as it would have to do it right initially. As we saw in Chapter 3, cheaping out on landscape grading will cost you even more later if it needs to be fixed because of all the other systems stacked on top of the grade platform. When I was an apprentice carpenter in my early twenties, Andy, the finish carpenter, told me something I never forgot. He told me if the foundation of the house is more than a fraction of an inch off, the carpenters have to adjust and fix the imperfection all the way through construction to the final trim work. The same premise applies to landscaping. You don't want to go back and redo the grade because you'll be faced with removing—and then redoing—all the top construction layers, including plumbing, pavers, sod and more.

Unfortunately, these kinds of grading problems are common. To create a proper grade—or correct a defective one—I use a mini excavator with a blade (like a small bulldozer), along with other machines and tools that allow me to work with nature. It might seem ironic that as someone sensitive to nature, I control and shape landscapes with earth-moving machines. In fact, the majority of the sites I work have been excavated before, so most of what

I'm doing is cleaning up and reorganizing materials left over from construction. I mainly dig through the remains to reveal the character of the place. Some places need retaining walls or rockeries for planting. Others need smoothing out and reconnecting disjointed pieces. Either way, even though I use powerful machines, I am careful to honor the place itself.

Using the right tool for the right job allows me to bring a site back to wholeness and balance. On a recent project, Sarah and I accomplished this with tactics that included grading, screening with trees and shrubs, and simplifying the functional living areas with the help of a variety of machines and tools. Our walk-behind Toro Dingo loader is a time- and back-saver. It weighs in at almost a ton, but can get through spaces as small as three feet wide. Moving material, digging, grading, sod removal, and carrying big trees are just a few of its uses. When different tool attachments are utilized, the Dingo really adds a wide range of possibilities.

On this job, however, it wouldn't quite fit through the small gate, so we used a wheel barrow to move compost and trees around to the back of the house. We also hired a conveyor truck to pump gravel over two fences for pathways and patio base material, which we later hand-raked. We were also able to use the Dingo to remove and load an old sod lawn into the pickup and haul it away.

Through strategic use of various tools and techniques, along with careful orchestration and check-ins with the owners, the project was completed in the most effective way. What was the key? We drove our actions with our goals and strategy, followed by the best available tactical means.

Machines expand landscape possibilities exponentially. Beyond the mowers, aerators, and thatchers used to maintain lawns, several powerful construction machines now expand the range of what can be done. I spend hundreds of hours a year operating a medium-size compact radius excavator. It has a bulldozer-type blade, but the main part is a hoe with a thumb for digging and grabbing big heavy items. I use my rubber track excavator to set boulders, grade, excavate, and process materials, though I've also used it for demolition of buildings, putting in utilities, dead tree removal and debris clean up.

As much as I love my machines, I also use plenty of hand tools in my work. By my count, I have over a dozen different types and size shovels alone, not to mention rakes, bars, pitch forks, etc. This is for someone who at age eighteen thought he'd go off to college for four years and never use a shovel again. I was sure wrong about that.

Of course, I also rely on my trusty pickup. Even if materials onsite are recycled and utilized for fill as a source of rock and topsoil, additional material will usually need to be purchased. The amount of material dictates whether I bring it in or hire a big trucking company to handle that part of the job. The guys who drive the big ten to twenty yard dump trucks can place material expertly and do so at very reasonable rates. One big load often adds up to more than a dozen pickup loads. In the final analysis, it's often less expensive to have someone else haul your material for you and much faster.

Machines aren't cheap, but neither is labor. An old myth and an ethnic slur says that most landscaping problems can be solved by "just getting a bunch of Mexicans to do it." That shows a client's true ignorance. Moving the really heavy material is beyond human strength, no matter how cheap or hard-working the workers are. The right machine can move heavy stuff and process material efficiently. Even if your crew can shovel dirt fast, the appropriate machine can "bury" them with speed and lift capability, and do things even the Inca or Egyptians couldn't.

But no machine—or crew, for that matter—will work well without the right person running it. The same goes for landscapes. Well-intentioned, uninformed and unskilled people, don't make for a good final project result. As I said earlier, laborers aren't craftsmen.

This difference between promise and delivery is no different with our American landscapes. The great ones actualized an original idea and implemented it correctly. When homeowners are talked into, or talk themselves into, doing a project based on a glossy image from a magazine, the result is almost never like the image. The same goes for finding a cheaper contactor. Once in a hundred times you'll get something for nothing, but those aren't good odds.

This isn't a new dilemma. Americans are dreamers. We inspire the world with people who turn dreams into reality. However, potential and actuality are not the same. One is an idea of the mind, the other a fact, a result in the world. A teenager I know well told me that he was really learning a lot and could easily get better grades. This may be true, but his actual GPA metric is the measure that matters when it comes to college hopes.

When you drive a stick shift, the steps you go through to translate the engine's power into the car taking you where you want to go require the transmission. This also holds true for building a great landscape. Even if you are armed with plans, proposals and pictures, someone still has to do the work. Manning the job, however, is just the start. Every landscape project, big or small, needs to be managed. Whether you're handling this yourself or hiring a pro, you'll need to stay on top of timing, resources and manpower. That's next.

Idea: Sometimes hiring someone rather than DIY can actually save you money.

Chapter 9

Managing the Job

You can't talk your way out of what you've behaved your way into.

—Stephen R. Covey

Managing the project starts with a clear concept of the process. Research first; discover by looking and listening. Even if you are very thorough and have plans drawn after this phase, new elements will be revealed during the excavation phase. I've yet to see a landscape that matches its two-dimensional plan, simply because the more you dig, the more you discover. If we stay alert, this naturally leads to using what we can from the excavation. As we've seen, the recycling phase involves sorting materials from the site, including boulders, dirt, fill, plants, and miscellaneous objects that are already on the property. Not only do you not have to haul them away, you don't have to bring in new materials to replace them. I've mentioned this simple concept before. I repeat it here because this one step will help you save the most money and allow you to do the best with what you've got to work with.

The final phase is all about adding, along with using what you have on hand for construction. You can now go shopping for materials, seed, plants, rock, gravel, and irrigation parts as needed. Once everything is onsite and mostly in place, you should give yourself extra time to complete the finish stage of your landscape. This is punch-list time, followed by clean up, but it's also when you solve the last of the nagging problems. Think of it as the difference between a manuscript's rough draft and a clean well-edited book for sale. It's the time to polish, or risk the remorse that comes with leaving a bunch of loose ends instead of completing the job.

Clarity about process will help you determine if you want to hire the work out or do it yourself. Either way, you'll be overseeing the job to some extent, so you'll want to pay attention to the information in this chapter.

If you've decided to hire someone to re-do your landscape, you should vet your potential contractor well before you hire him or her. A fancy web site and fake enthusiasm can often end up selling a bid with an undefined result. I had to rescue one client after a contractor "friend of the family" had been fired. The contractor had left behind a huge pile from dozens of truckloads of rock and dirt intended for a rockery and had squandered so much of the clients' budget on all that material that it took them three more years to complete their original project. In the end, the yard got fenced for small children and almost all the money spent on rock and dirt proved a waste. In this case, a fancy website and big talk even from an established contractor who the clients knew personally did not equal a good result.

It's no wonder that people usually put in a generic "cheap" landscape just to be safe. Later, they add plants and more from the big box stores out of habit and because products are readily available. The approach, however "safe" and familiar, is another big trap, because it starts from the wrong premise.

As you now know, the best built landscapes start with research, then removal (excavation), next recycling. Adding is the fourth phase just before finally finishing. The big problem is that most people start by buying—the adding phase—and skip the rest.

Launch your landscape with a good plan or use a contractor who's willing to create a viable plan to meet your needs and make the most of your property. Someone will ultimately have to deal with your landscape's challenges—a slick salesman is probably not your best bet on this front. Negotiating and selling skill sets aren't what's needed to get the work done—management is required. In addition, since there usually is back and forth between owners and the contractor during construction, defining who is doing what at the outset is a must. Skipping this step will cost you one way or another. Finally, whether you or someone you hire is making decisions about your landscaping, you need to make sure that you consider your desired end result in every decision you make.

A project that involved a steep hillside lot with a proposed backyard living area off the house was to be "managed" by the customer. Aside from the customer, the biggest problem with this job was the elevations. 20 or 25 percent extra to build the backyard right seemed extravagant to this prospect, so I lost the bid. He decided against doing the excavation. As a result, the stairs he was forced to add in order to get to and from the living area ended up swallowing up half the space, and more of the budget than he expected. The new backyard had been intended for entertaining. It would have been a great place for a water feature that would be visible from the house and could have tied the space together nicely. However, water features need to be in the ground, not on top of the grade, and because the needed excavation wasn't done, the final water feature didn't end up looking like it was part of the place. The yard this prospect ended up with was a cosmetic improvement over an empty lot, but not optimal for his desired socializing.

If you want a hardscape that works, you have to explore what you really want and need before settling on a cheap superficial solution that neglects the correct process for success. What's the worth of a backyard built mainly for guests if it winds up being half the original size and feels cramped after unnecessary, expensive and potentially hazardous stairs have been installed?

Whether you're doing the work or hiring out, you'll be making constant choices about what should be done, as well as about when to do it. Getting fixated on sticking to the rules brings frustration, but if you don't know the rules you'll find yourself way out of pocket or behind schedule before you've even started.

Half the battle to complete a project involves getting all the supplies, parts and tools onsite. The landscape contractor who taught me irrigation was always running to the store to pick up a fitting or to get some glue. His reasoning was "I get paid by the hour so why not drive around town for awhile?" As for the guys with cell phones implanted in their heads, they seem to think, "What's the big urgency to order materials? We can always order what we need when we need it after we get the bid approved."

That's not how I see it. When I give a bid to a client to approve I have already secured materials and the help I'll need. Then, as the customer looks over the bid, I call for the locates (they mark up the locations of underground utilities). I also clean up any other responsibilities, so that once the proposal is accepted I can devote my entire attention to the project. The time to have materials delivered is just before you are ready to use them. Sometimes you'll need more of a particular material or something unexpected will come up. Things happen, but every sizable job needs a legal bid/contract so that everyone involved knows what's included and expected. Don't start off your job with change orders and additions; this is a sure sign that someone isn't thinking right.

Once begun, work needs to flow and so does money. Starting a job without planning for cash flow will negatively impact the project outcome. Once people get fixated on money and paychecks instead of on work-related problems, you can be sure that the quality of their work will go down. Doing a job just for the money takes the fun out of it, but if "money is not an issue" trust me, it will become one in a way you won't like.

You also won't get good bang for your buck if you spend your money having a lot of people around and pass it out like candy or expect the job to take longer than necessary simply because you feel you paid a hefty fee. If you go to a dentist, you don't tell him to bring in more assistants or take twice the time he needs to because you are paying a lot for the work. The same goes for landscapes. Taking more time and having more bodies on the job isn't the goal. The right size crew is different depending on the project, but if you pay for attention and activity you are off track.

You must know what you want, and then manage yourself. Make sure your contractor or your crew understand your objectives. Even on the smallest construction projects, management is a factor that will affect your results. Having helpers or subs come part but not all of the week can be the best of both worlds. No laborer likes to be sent home mid-day, so respect that he or she showed up to work and provide a full day's work if possible. As always, this is why you want to communicate well, have meetings and stay on the same page by planning ahead.

Weeding out bad apples and unqualified individuals is your most important management task. If you have people around who are chatterboxes—or worse yet, substance abusers— you must eliminate them from your job site. Neurotic talk or mindless action won't help. If any of your workers are "spaced out," lose them. Send them somewhere else for their fun and games, but don't let them distract you from your job. You want things to flow smoothly and the work at hand to get done right on your time schedule. Just like the landscape itself, start by eliminating whatever doesn't work.

Make time your ally, so that it really is on your side. On a job site, there are busy times and slow times during the week and day. If you're running the show, use the opportunities given to you to get the work done. If it's hard to think and lay out an irrigation system with the crew mulling around, get to the job early. Better yet, line up your system layout after most of them leave. Then you can sleep on it and you'll be ready for a fresh start the next day.

In between stubbornness and a free spirit lies flexibility. If it's raining and you'd planned to work on a roof, you change your plans. If half the crew takes off to a big ball game or rock show, don't do their work for them. If the stone you ordered suddenly isn't available, find a substitute that you like even better. Adjust and stay focused on the big picture.

When things come up that you don't expect, having order within the context of your work week will ease these disruptions. Mondays almost always have something frustrating to offer. Build in some shock absorbers, set your meetings for later if they aren't urgent, and do things that keep you out of Monday's crosshairs.

On Friday, people aren't concentrating on work and peel off early. This is the wrong time to take on risky critical tasks. If you need to dig up a water main, do it on a day when you have time to fix things if they don't go as planned. In keeping with the Friday mindset, do smaller tasks that have easier closure.

Friday is also a good day to clean up and leave an organized job site for weekend enjoyment, and so you can start your work week fresh. As progress moves along, I like to check in with my clients weekly. I want a snapshot still frame, not a blurry mess that's hard to decipher when they check it. By ending and starting the week with the job site re-organized and cleaned up, tools and equipment parked, etc., it'll make sense to them, too. You may not fall into the five-day work-week scenario. In that case, working on Saturday is better than overdoing it on Friday.

Landscapes reflect the people involved in building them. Construction is a process of adding the skills and propensities that those involved bring to the table. We are all creatures of habit and are more set in our ways then we probably want to admit. For instance, one type of personality is super organized. This kind of person gets into the smallest detail to the point of distraction from the big picture result desired. A landscape that has "everything" covered—neatly placed bark chips, planting beds or lawn edged with a cement curb or plastic strip—is evidence of a detail person. The other personality extreme is expressed by a wild free-for-all of separate projects within the yard going in different directions. Whatever your work style, you want to balance out the extremes so you don't end up with someone else's art therapy project. The state of the current landscape reflects the underlying state of mind of those who have left their mark on it. It's a lot like reading body language. Managing personalities gracefully improves outcomes.

As you move forward with a project, personalities directly impact the choices that get made before and during construction. Here's the rub: even if you are able to tune into tendencies that will be counterproductive, you still have to be proactive to help neutralize them. Just recognizing that you are impatient or rash in your judgments doesn't change your habit. Even if you put some effort into it, it's probably wishful thinking to expect yourself—or others involved in the project— to change. Creating counter-balance with your landscaping team just may prove more practical.

Using less ego and more intelligent choices will help you find your effectiveness zone. I've seen where a big picture thinker can miss details and underestimate costs. By having a detail person share both design and implementation decisions, you're more likely to end up with a healthy balance and superior landscape.

Thinking ahead and having someone with experience to guide the process will pay off in far less emotional upheaval. The flow of a project is a little like a concert or a play with different acts or scenes. In the end, if the parts work together the result will show it. This is a case where the whole is greater than the sum of the parts. After you have a plan, you dig into the job, starting at the beginning, and chew your way through it.

The work comes in layers, with each phase of the project having its particular issues that need attention. The beginning is for getting parts and materials set up and onsite. It's for getting sub contractors, workers, and clients' responsibilities outlined. The middle of a project should have work flowing and moving, a productive rhythm of building. This is the worst time to take the crew somewhere else to deal with some other project or task. The end needs to be about finishing and details, including fixing any mistakes left from the faster-paced middle of the project, and using up or removing the leftover materials. Then clean up, polish, and take your after pictures.

You can use different metaphors for landscaping—you either attack the work or you heal the site. Either way, you must keep clear intention and attention on the task at hand. During each phase of the landscaping process, the work itself is the most important focus; it should be your Zen. Cell phones can save you time and keep you in touch, but they can also distract from getting work done and staying focused at the job site. Building happens on the project site, not on the phone. If you or your contractor can immerse yourselves in the work, it'll get done right and without delay. Limiting distractions from second-rate workers, neighboring activities and unclear instructions helps. When a layer of work is complete, go ahead and take a break, examine what you've accomplished and look it over for any additional tweaks it might need. Better to take care of any of these details immediately while they're fresh and easier to access. Don't be in a hurry to cover up something before you test it or examine it.

In the end, you want your project to have a personality. It should have some artistic zest to it. Zest and passion won't come through the work if you are not successfully managing the personalities involved during construction. You also need to know when to step out of the way when you have the right people on the right tasks. Nobody wants to be micromanaged; it takes the fun and pride out of their work.

When a job flows and people are proud of their contributions, the results reflect that. The project will take just the right time to complete and you'll get the best from the workers' skills and expertise. There is a sweet spot where the work is fun, timeless, and meaningful. People want to show up to the job. When workers with this kind of attitude build a landscape, the end result can even give you goose bumps.

Idea: Correctly managing the timing of your job will make the process more efficient and save you money.

Chapter 10

It's Easy to Lose Money Landscaping

*So you have to lick the honey
from between the thorns.*

L osing money on landscaping is easy. Maximizing your results, while simple, isn't easy.

It's natural to resist change, even when what we are doing is wrong and we know better. I recently learned that the U.S. military is starting to adopt green sustainable energy tactics. They currently spend billions of dollars on fuel to power air-conditioned camps in the war zones. Attacks on the tank trucks that carry fuel used for this air-conditioning are responsible for a big number of casualties since the trucks are prime targets for the roadside bombers. Simply using insulating foam on the camp tents (thus substantially reducing air conditioning needs) has proven to pay back its cost in just sixty days. In one case, the insulation saved the military $95 million. The old way is clearly a losing proposition. Yet the military has yet to adopt these sustainable techniques on a large scale.

You can fault bureaucracy; after all, the U.S. military is a big one. However, the status quo is sticky and any real progress is often slower than we expect. So don't lose hope, especially where your own landscape is concerned. Recognizing your own status quo resistances and the blind spots that we all have is a helpful, open place to work from. Your own blind spots and status quo, however, aren't obvious, but figuring them out is worth the effort. Habits are hard enough to change, but without recognizing them first, finding a more effective way to go about things has about the same odds of success as winning the lottery.

I've shared landscaping techniques in these pages where green change will pay off in real dollars. The challenge, once you've been educated, is to keep moving and start implementing the changes you know you can and you should make. This is probably the hardest part. Use some psychology on yourself. As the carrot, think of the money you can save. For the stick, think of how you'll feel if you spend thousands of dollars for no good reason.

Unless you're able to witness and test what we've been talking about in this book, your own determination to move with a changed approach will often be frustrated. My suggestion is to tour landscapes using sustainable methods. Go see them for yourself and explore the feel of the space. You might even try out techniques and practices in a class. The same holds true if you want to hire out the work. Make sure you see previous work and talk to the contractors' past clients. Landscape isn't like heart surgery where getting it wrong kills you. However, it's very easy for the uninformed to misjudge what the end result will really be.

As a contractor for most of my life, I've made plenty of mistakes and I still get an occasional ego enema. However, in my role as a design and project consultant I have witnessed even more pain, frustration and wasted money in the projects I fix for others. After so many years spent upgrading landscapes, I have a kind of x-ray vision and see the problems that plague just about every landscape. All landscapes have problems that fall somewhere on a continuum from nuisance to nightmare. But you can get it mostly right from the outset if you follow a logical progression before and during construction. If you only take away a single idea from this entire book, here's my #1 money-saving tip: Subtract before you add.

Most landscape contractors and customers think that landscaping is a matter of addition only. They are wrong! Three steps should precede adding products and materials—studying, emptying space, and recycling.

Admittedly these three ideas aren't big sellers. We're all feeling the strong pull of consumerism. Marketers live on selling the sizzle, not the steak. It's no different buying landscape products. Mom-and-Pop businesses and the big box stores sure have stuff to sell you and me. But if you want more for your money, resist your urge to buy stuff first.

But wait. You'll also receive . . . more of what *you* really value.

Recycle on-site materials and plants before adding any significant new materials or products to your landscape. During excavation for your project, you need to get rid of all the unwanted elements. Debris and faulty structures need to be eliminated, not just built around as is often done by adding only. As materials are removed, sort for future use and haul unusable debris to the dump. But save any existing assets that can be re-used on site for final use during rebuilding.

Even before you excavate and recycle, you'll want to research. As an initial step, develop a plan from what you find on site. List and/or mark what should be saved and what gets taken out. It's important to mark up underground utilities, existing irrigation and lighting, etc. This is also the time to section off those areas you want to leave native. It's a lot easier and cheaper to protect a natural area than try to re-create it later.

So first, research your site and match it with your needs. Second, eliminate the structures that don't serve the project. Next, sort materials and recycle where possible. Finally, put your landscape together and rebuild it the way you want it to be. This construction part of the landscaping process has been discussed in detail elsewhere. The difference here is that now you are using a kind of site alchemy to utilize resources you have on and in the site. This also naturally promotes a design that is sensitive to the place.

In short, the steps are:

- Research
- Remove
- Recycle
- Rebuild

Rock, trees, plants, and dirt shouldn't be wasted. The native balance and personality of the place, if blended with the new construction, will simplify and improve your natural design.

All landscapes have histories that pre-date your arrival on the scene. If you've ever driven old highways like route 99 or 66, you've seen the pre-interstate highway system. The buildings and remnants of older businesses are like a time capsule offering a glimpse of the past. Learning your property's history provides similar insights. You can discover the history of ownership when studying the title company's closing documents, city or county septic system plans, and paperwork from the original building plans. Observation can fill in other blanks. A property I once owned was very near an old Indian camping spot. I figured that out through observation and conversations with some long-time residents. Finding arrowheads was another good clue.

You probably won't fall in love with research. However, shifting to this kind of observational landscape research can be very simple and even playful. For instance, I use water to clean away edges of sidewalks and driveways so I can clearly see the lines and composition of the project. Like dinosaur bone hunters who wait for big rain storms before they search for the bones, when you wash away dust and debris, you will find treasures underneath.

Properties, like over packed closets, accumulate finished and unfinished projects. Most happen incrementally and are not well planned. Observational research will help you sort out the "fingerprints" left there from the past. In this way, you'll have a better read on what you'll really be working with when you start landscape construction.

Research also includes the reading you've been doing with this book. (Good work!) Other programs, classes and professionals in the trades can help you sort out your site's unique story. Don't ever be afraid to ask experts for information. Go ahead, I give you permission to shake them down for answers. Your question might just be the best compliment they get that day. Get into the thought process of those who did the previous work on the property you are now modifying or fixing. Research is walking in others' shoes, creating rapport and paying attention. Do it first and save money. This same kind of education will also help you select a contractor to recreate or enhance your landscape, should that be of interest. Contractors who last will listen to their clients and read them like they read the site. As a customer, speaking the language of design and contracting gives you an advantage.

In the old days, many homeowners would do their due diligence by interviewing three contractors out of the phone book. Now many hire a designer to draw up a plan. Others tour gardens or landscapes that turned out well. The Internet has tons of information and is a great tool.

All this information is helpful, but only if it gives you the actual knowledge you need to get results. Depending on the scale of your project, take the appropriate time to understand what you will be faced with and consider your realistic options. Research is very cheap compared to the problems and mistakes it will save you from. It's like inexpensive prevention compared to the high cost of a cure. Consider it similar to insurance, but in this case you get paid back by *not* having accidents.

I am often critical of generic-style landscapes because they never work with the property and its personality. Research will add dimension as well as a dose of sustainability to your project, and ensure that you avoid a generic result. Michelangelo said, "Every block of stone has a statue inside it and it is the task of the sculptor to discover it." So dig in and uncover all the layers of the onion. When you start to cry, you're on the right track. Okay, enough metaphors; sorry, I just couldn't resist.

Great landscapes start with sensitive excavation. This means removing what isn't part of the final work and recycling any and all materials for later use. Don't be shy; do the excavation if it's needed. Just make sure you've tagged, painted and marked what stays and what goes. Excavators or backhoes are blunt instruments and need clear direction even with an expert operator. Mark with paint, landscape flags or stakes so the operators can see everything from inside their machines.

Recycled junk rock (the little ones) or the jagged bigger pieces can be put in the future fill material pile. Nice boulders—especially the ones with lichen and moss growth—need to be carefully saved. Save any other interesting boulders for use in retaining walls or rockeries. Your equipment operator can sort through and organize if you ask him to. When dealing with this kind of more intricate excavation work, you want an experienced person at the controls. This isn't the time to rent a machine (mini excavator or backhoe) for your first time. All too often, material gets trampled, trucked out or simply lost in the shuffle. Recycling takes someone with skill in organizing as well as running the equipment. Ultimately, you probably won't be able to reuse all excavated materials. Most contractors, however, don't even try to use any. They just haul everything off and bring in what they need later, usually at a big cost to the owner.

It's been said that a problem well defined is a problem half solved. Landscaping is a little like putting together a jigsaw puzzle—it gets easier as you have fewer pieces to choose from. If you know it's got to go, eliminating the junk from your work site sooner will speed the job along. Just make sure you don't haul away most of what you could use later.

Recycling plants is different from recycling the site materials. Plants don't like being moved, especially when they are pushing their new growth. So move them in early spring or fall if you can. They also don't like being dug up and then not replanted quickly. If you can dig them out and replant the same day, you'll get the best results.

Follow a good planting recipe and don't let roots dry out.

At the rebuild stage, you've got a canvas to work with and materials from the site are organized for later when rebuilding. You will have a clear sense now of how much dirt, rock and other construction materials to buy at this point. The project's parameters will be much better defined at this stage too.

It is a little more complicated to manage both materials already onsite and materials brought in. But once you hit the rebuild stage, everything will be placed somewhere new anyway. Whether you are building up a grade, terracing a hill, or simply building a berm, work from big to small just as you would if you had a sanding project. You start with the heavier grit sand paper, and then use a finer and finer grit.

Once you establish rough grades by distributing the materials, the steps, water features and fire pits, along with outdoor kitchen or shower/tubs, should start to get roughed in. Big trees can go in at this point as well.

I wait for final grade to install lawns, patios, and plumbing for lawn irrigation. After the space is defined by these elements, run your drip as you do final plantings. Finally, you can top with ground cover and do finishing touches.

There's a big payoff if you wait to add until you've completed the research, remove and recycle steps. Your landscape will work better and be worth more in real dollars. So the next time you think about quickly adding lawn—or anything else—to your landscape, just stop. Slow down, take a little time and consider your design goals before you buy anything.

Trial and error is my #2 money waster in landscape construction. You don't really see the final product until it's done (or in many cases, when it can't seem to get finished). Unlike a car or an RV, you can't take it back to the dealer or resell it. Maybe that's why so many people test the waters with little projects before tackling their whole landscape. But as you've learned from this book, this piecemeal approach is less than successful.

Thinking that habits are easy to change is mistake #3. Those who think the learning curve doesn't apply to them are doomed to repeat their mistakes. But finding a new way may not be easy to do. In fact, doing things differently means you might even get worse at them before you get better. We really have to break with the past in order to break through.

The true road to skill starts with recognizing our own incompetence in a particular area. Being aware of our own lack of information or skill vaporizes this "ignorance is bliss" mode. Only when we are aware can we then learn the needed skills. Once we do a job the right way for enough time, our conscious mind gives that knowledge over to the unconscious. This stage, called mastery or unconscious competency, is the result of doing something "ten thousand times." And that's exactly why I enlist the help of experts. I know I'm a slow learner, but together with other experts, great results are indeed possible. Use your strengths, but don't be afraid to take a chance once in a while and try something new. If running equipment or installing plumbing interest you, go ahead and start along the learning curve. Just manage your expectations and then enjoy the education process.

I know I can't transfer my years of work experience in a short book. If I can give you two or three ideas for your landscape, I'll feel I've provided the value I promised. I'm a landscape contractor who personally works his projects with the help of subcontractors instead of employees. So my approach is more like a property owner's than a company with a big crew and overhead. I've picked key points for you to consider and tried to let you into my own thinking process in order to give you a sense of the work and how I do it. Hopefully my shared experiences will help you achieve landscaping results that honor your property as much as your own lifestyle.

That reminds me of the story of the wise old farmer and the preacher. A man of God is walking down the lane when he stops to talk with a farmer in front of his farm. The preacher remarks on the bounty and beauty of the farmer's place. "What an abundant and amazing gift from God," he says. The farmer directs the preacher's attention to the property next door that's empty and in disrepair. "That's what my farm looked like before, when God had it all to himself." The moral of the story: nature won't do it all by herself.

I'm not judge, jury, or the ultimate expert. My intention is to give you great tools to improve your landscape project and to save you money...just what I promised you to start with. My own thinking evolved during the writing of this book. The three key concepts of expansiveness, authenticity, and process are what I want you to take away as positive points of view. This book's title changed from *A Landscape of Ultimate Simplicity* to *Ultimate Simple Landscaping*. I changed the title to make it easier for you to remember these three key points.

Ultimate is bigger, open, and expansive. It's your best option(s). It's what you'd do if you couldn't fail. It's infinite. It's big picture thinking that focuses on concept before details.

Simple is the essence, which is actually harder in the short term. Long-term simple, however, is golden. If you are working too hard for some future

155

payoff, maybe consider simplifying what you are doing. Simple is unique, it's what is true for a specific place and/or person. Elegant systems, including nature, provide simplicity

I chose *Landscaping* rather than *Landscape* because your system of landscaping determines your landscape result. Nature and people continually influence all landscapes, so the processes, rhythms, and cycles are in motion and never static. Landscaping involves working with a moving target. There can be a Zen experience (time perception change) to your work. In the east, work is dharma (your calling). However, not respecting the process and focusing only on the cheapest results takes the fun, beauty, and value out of the pursuit. Attitude and approach bring real results.

By building a sustainable landscape you'll be rewarded in both money savings and livability. The ultimate buy-local campaign can start with you "buying" usable materials and native plants from yourself first. Even if there really is zero global warming and man hasn't polluted or in other ways impacted this globe negatively, you'll still get much more for your investment when you build landscapes using the principles outlined in this book. And if we *are* degrading the earth and environment for our children and their children (and ourselves) with our continuing unsustainable energy-wasting habits, you can help make a difference by going green. So go for it, have some fun along the way, create some beautiful landscapes that fit your property and your life, and put money back into your own pocket in the process.

Idea: *Remember—the future is never what it used to be.*

Conclusion

Get Twice as Much for Your Money (or, Buy Everything at Half the Price)

It's true that if you can pay half as much as you would have or get twice as much for your money, you've just doubled your buying power. As consumers, we have to appreciate that equation. In these pages I've shared simple ideas that translate into straightforward landscape construction techniques that every day do just that for my clients.

As I finish this book, economic times have been strange and tight. Even though property prices have fallen off a cliff here in Bend, the town is alive. Every day and night, life goes on. I believe that this trying period is yet another call to get creative and solve our problems. Because money itself is often the biggest problem, I've shared my expertise about saving money in landscape construction. No matter how native you go, landscaping will never be free. No matter how much you shave the price, great landscapes will never be cheap. No good investment is without cost. However, if your dollars buy you twice as much because of your own intelligent and informed choices, you can take that to the bank.

Ultimate simple landscaping starts with realizing that when landscapes are treated like sculpture we live in, over time and with love and money added, they can transform into naturally beautiful gardens. I haven't wanted to confuse the issue by differentiating between the words *landscape* and *garden*, but I can no longer resist. For me, gardens are landscapes with something extra that takes them beyond the superficial or ordinary. An old growth stand of trees with natural clear springs and mother logs is a garden to me. Botanical gardens like the Oregon gardens in Silverton are often spiritual and relaxing places to experience with all your senses. For further inspiration, check out Ken Burns' documentary on our national parks—landscaping on a grand, and quintessentially American, scale.

Landscapes—whether large or small, public or private—that honor the place and enrich those who experience them can be considered gardens. I'm not talking here about the ad in the real estate section that offers a "park-like setting," but rather gardens that evolve with you throughout your life. My clients Cindy and Homer Hepworth have worked on their landscape for decades. Each time it gets better. They didn't spend a fortune doing it, either. Cindy's had the work done in stages and in layers. Over time, they have enjoyed both the process and result of sculpting their landscape. They know that as beautiful as any garden/landscape is, it will change over time. Honoring that dimension of time and leaving their stamp on their space has resulted in a garden/landscape that truly reflects and enriches their lives.

I wish the same for you and your landscape. It's been my privilege to write this book. Thank you for your interest.

The Green/Sustainability movement is starting to meld and merge with the tight money times. Destroying the Planet little by little with bad habits of consumption is meeting up with tighter restrictions and higher costs. For instance the price of water is going up and will continue to do so. So wasting money on ugly landscapes and paying to maintain them is out. Times change, and in this book you'll find low tech innovations that are ahead of the curve. I promise you understandable ideas in simple steps.

The Landscape industry includes Landscape Maintenance, Landscape Architects, Landscape Suppliers and what I do; landscape building. Specifically I construct architectural, (sculptural type) landscapes. I also help with design as described here in these pages. Landscaping for more than 40 years, now, much about the business has changed. The cast of characters has grown. Today we have more sources of Landscape supply, more style choices and much more involvement from clients. However the role players—designers, suppliers, maintenance, clients and builders remain the same.

In *Ultimate Simple Landscaping* I sell my point of view as a builder/designer. Honestly, to the point and in word picture format. More like the language of contracts than photos or site plans. It's the story of techniques, ideas, and perspectives that I use for best results. It identifies what landscaping matters most and it's focused on helping you get better results when designing and building your landscape.

For portfolio pictures, more resources or information on our book 55 Myth, Tips, and Secrets: Bend's Essential Guide to Landscaping. Check our website

Fred Swisher

Bendpinenursery.com